TUSCARAWAS COUNTY
MURDER & MAYHEM

TUSCARAWAS COUNTY MURDER & MAYHEM

NOEL B. POIRIER

THE History PRESS

Published by The History Press
An imprint of Arcadia Publishing
Charleston, SC
www.historypress.com

First published 2025

Manufactured in the United States

ISBN 9781467159661

Library of Congress Control Number: 2025941987

CONTENTS

PREFACE

Tuscarawas County, Ohio's history is full of the same criminal and tragic history to be found in the history of any other community in the United States. The stories found in this volume have been gleaned from local newspaper accounts from the Tuscarawas County community and throughout the state of Ohio. Oftentimes the names of individuals are misspelled by the press, and especially so when the names were of recent immigrants to the area. The author has decided to be consistent in the spelling and, when public records were available, used the spelling found on those documents. Quotes related to the stories that follow come from the various newspaper accounts of the events and to the attributed individuals noted by the newspaper reporters. These newspaper accounts were accessed using the websites newspapers.com, newspaperarchive.com, genealogybank.com, archive.org and loc.gov.

The multitude of sources utilized in the telling of these tales of murder and mayhem are historical newspapers, as mentioned above, public records and genealogical resources readily available to the author from sources such as familysearch.org, ancestry.com, fold3.com and similar genealogical sites. When possible, effort has been made to provide some family history for the individuals named, including birth and death dates for individuals mentioned in the stories. To footnote every instance of source material would require twice the number of pages to document, so footnotes have been excluded. Any errors are the author's alone.

1873

MURDER OF TUSCARAWAS COUNTY'S DYAS MILLS IN COLORADO

Jonathan Winn Mills (1813–1869) was born in Virginia and around the age of twenty left his native state and moved to Ohio with a couple of his brothers. The Mills brothers at first settled in the area that became Carroll County, where, in 1834, Jonathan married Ohio-born Sarah Downing (1813–1898). The Millses then moved to the town of New Cumberland, Warren Township, in Tuscarawas County by 1840. There Jonathan and Sarah acquired farmland just to the east of town, became active in local politics and raised what would become a very large family.

Jonathan and Sarah had eleven children over the course of their marriage—eight sons and three daughters—of which eight would survive to adulthood. Jonathan's political activity, and apparent popularity, resulted in him being elected to represent Tuscarawas County in the Ohio state legislature in the 1850s. Meanwhile, his farm continued to prosper and expand with the assistance of his family and the other laborers who worked on his farm. The Millses were Republicans, and during the American Civil War, at least two of the sons served with an Ohio regiment during the war.

After the war, a couple of Jonathan and Sarah's sons moved to Illinois while the other children continued to live on the family farm in Tuscarawas County. Jonathan Mills, while returning from a trip to Mineral Point in November 1869, was thrown from his buggy and suffered fatal injuries as a result. He lived long enough though to write his will, leaving the property to his widow and naming his son James as the executor of his estate. James decided to buy out his siblings' remaining interest in the family farm, and using that money and the portion of the estate they inherited, two of the brothers decided to start a new life in the West; those two brothers were Thomas (1838–1912) and Dyas Mills (1848–1873).

The elder of the two brothers, Thomas, married Elizabeth McGregor (1840–aft. 1879) in 1857 and, by the time of Jonathan's death in 1869, was farming in Warren Township with his wife and four children. Dyas, meanwhile, was living on the family farm with his mother and two other siblings. Thomas and Dyas decided, shortly after their brother bought out their share of the family farm in 1870 or so, to relocate to the territory of Colorado. Thomas, his family and his brother Dyas packed up their belongings and headed west, settling in the town of Kiowa, southeast of Denver. There Thomas purchased a ranch about a mile outside of town, and the two brothers started their new life in the West.

During the winter of 1873, Dyas determined to go on a buffalo and antelope hunt on the plains to the east of Kiowa. Given that it was Dyas's first winter hunt of this kind, his older brother furnished him with everything he needed for the hunt and arranged for one of the family ranch hands to go along with him. The ranch hand was an Apache named Charley, who was also a friend of Dyas's. Now outfitted with a wagon and horse, blankets, guns and ammunition, the two men headed east onto the plains the day after Christmas 1873 in search of game. After a few days of hunting, the men decided to take the antelope they had managed to acquire to the nearest town to sell.

It was around eight o'clock in the evening on New Year's Eve when Dyas and Charley arrived in the small town of River Bend that sat along a stretch of the Kansas Pacific Railroad. The men had already started drinking before they arrived in town, and their first stop was a store and saloon where they sold the antelope they had shot that day. Dyas then ordered some whiskey for himself, and Charley demanded a drink as well. Dyas jokingly told him to drink from a water pail on the bar, but Charley continued to demand whiskey. Charley then went to the wagon to grab a rifle, and Dyas and the others in the saloon soon followed. Charley was outside by the wagon, rifle in hand, demanding whiskey and threatening Dyas and the other men.

Dyas, moving toward Charley, told him to calm down and that he could get whiskey or anything else he wanted when they went back inside. Before Charley could move, though, Dyas grabbed the rifle out of his hands and slammed the butt of it into Charley's face. Charley fell to the ground and crawled under the wagon for protection as Dyas continued to try to get to him. The other men with Dyas grabbed the rifle out of his hands and, when Dyas tried to reach for a board to hit Charley with, managed to keep that away from him as well. The other men managed to calm Dyas down, and they started to walk back into the saloon. Charley crawled out from under the wagon and ran toward Dyas with his nine-inch-long hunting knife and plunged it into Dyas's back, between his left shoulder blade and spine. Dyas fell to the ground and yelled, "He has killed me!"

Dyas Mills lay on the saloon floor, bleeding profusely from the stab wound, as one man tried to sew up his wound and another ran for the town sheriff. The other men in the saloon grabbed Charley and tied him up until the sheriff arrived. Once the sheriff arrived and it became clear that Dyas would not live, he feared that the men at the saloon would lynch Charley and determined to take Charley on the very next train to Denver for safekeeping until a hearing could be held the next day. The following afternoon, Charley was brought back to River Bend for his hearing; traveling in the same train car with him was Thomas Mills. The two men did not speak.

The hearing was a brief one, and as news of the murder of Dyas Mills spread, an even larger mob gathered in the small town. After the conclusion of the hearing, Charley was once again placed on a train bound for the jail in Denver for his own safekeeping. However, on their arrival in Denver, the sheriff was told that there was not enough room in the jail for Charley and he would have to be moved to another jail. During the move to the Douglas County Jail in Castle Rock, unknown persons took Charley from the jail, and he was later found hanging from a tree "being hung by unknown persons."

Thomas, in the meantime, brought his brother Dyas's body back to be buried at the ranch outside Kiowa. Thomas did not stay in Colorado very long after the death of his brother. His wife divorced him in 1879, and Thomas eventually found himself living, with a new wife, in eastern Oklahoma, where he died in 1912. Dyas's name is listed on a headstone in the New Cumberland Cemetery in Tuscarawas County, though there is no evidence that his body returned to Ohio. There are many records online that record Dyas's death as having occurred in 1878, but his actual death occurred in the early morning hours of January 1, 1874, in a small town in Colorado, 1,300 miles from home.

1878
A MURDER IN PORT WASHINGTON

John Stull (1828–1910) was born in Ohio, the son of Michael Stull Jr. (1801–c. 1880) and his wife, Catherine Hohn (1799–1903). John, in his youth, served in Company C of the Fourth Ohio Volunteer Infantry during the Mexican War. When he returned from service, he first appears in Tuscarawas County's 1850 census living in his father's household in Salem Township. He married seventeen-year-old neighbor Catherine Renneker (1839–1924) in 1856, began farming and started to raise a large family of his own.

When, and how, John Stull learned the art and science of distilling spirits is not known. Though it should be noted that, like their southern neighbors in Kentucky, Ohio farmers were well versed in the process of converting grain to alcohol. It was essential for farmers who lived any great distance from a population center to find other ways to sell their crops. The Stull family owned around eighty acres of land northwest of Port Washington, roughly where current West Hill Road crosses over Interstate 77 along Buckhorn Creek.

Where exactly John Stull established his distillery is not clear. His advertisement, in December 1870, that announced its establishment states that it was in Port Washington, but it is also possible that it was on their property outside of the town itself. The latter seems more likely when one considers how later events were reported. While there were a number of distillery fires in the early 1870s, John Stull's distillery was luckily spared that fate and thrived.

Management of John Stull's distillery changed hands in 1874, though the name stayed the same and John continued to work in the distillery. The new management advertised that they had "pure rye whiskey" for sale and offered whiskey as payment for grain. A newspaper article referencing the distillery, published in the fall of 1878, distracted me from the history of distilling in Tuscarawas County and took the story of John Stull in a very different direction.

It was Sunday, November 10, 1878, when someone came across the body of a woman about two miles from Port Washington, her neck broken and her body beaten badly. The person who found the body recognized it as a local widow named Amy Best (1823–1878). The news hit the New Philadelphia press the following Thursday, November 14, and an investigation into her death was underway. It did not take long for the investigation to uncover the murderer.

On Friday, November 9, Catherine Stull went to the distillery looking for her husband, John, and was told that he was out in the distillery's hog lot. On reaching the lot, she saw her husband on a hill near the residence of Amy Best. He was tearing up a piece of paper that he had removed from under a rock. She confronted John and accused him of having an affair with the widow Best. He denied the affair and ordered Catherine to return home.

When Catherine returned home, she wrote a note to Best, pretending to be John, asked to meet her the following day and left the note under the stone on the hill. The next day, at the allotted time and place, Catherine confronted Best about having an affair with her husband. The information on what happened next, for obvious reasons, relies entirely on the testimony of Catherine Stull.

According to Catherine's confession, "Mrs. Best immediately came toward her in a menacing attitude, and that she [Catherine] struck Mrs. Best with a club in self-defence [*sic*]; and then tried to choke her, failing in which, she picked her up and threw, or pushed her over the fence and down the hill." The case against Catherine was clear-cut: she had confessed, and she was subsequently arrested and jailed.

There is no record of how much time Catherine spent in the county jail leading up to her case reaching a county grand jury in late January 1879. When the grand jury completed their deliberations regarding Catherine's killing of Amy Best, they decided not to indict Stull on any charges. She left the courthouse a free woman on February 6, 1879. According to newspaper accounts, the grand jury determined that there was no way to obtain a conviction of Catherine Stull and that the cost of a trial was not warranted. Apparently, the grand jury felt that she had been driven to her crime by the actions of her husband and Best.

One newspaper reported that the community "rejoiced" over the grand jury's decision, but the press did not. Editorials in a number of papers excoriated the grand jury for releasing a confessed murderer. One paper reported that "she [Catherine Stull] is at liberty now to use her club, and beat out the brains of some other helpless being." Another paper accused the grand jury of valuing a woman's life less than a man's, stating, "If, however, the clubbing process was applied to another sex, perhaps, even some grand jurors might see things in a different light." Catherine Stull, by her own admission, had murdered Amy Best but was never tried for the crime.

Catherine would return to her husband and family. Perhaps escaping her murderous past, the couple relocated to Hamilton County, Ohio, after 1880. They were living with their son Samuel and his family in Cincinnati in 1900. The couple are buried in Glen Haven Cemetery in Harrison, Ohio.

1881

THE BODY SNATCHING OF JOHN ROLL

The clandestine removal of corpses from burial sites, or "body snatching," was a common practice during the nineteenth century. The goal of the snatchers, or "resurrectionists," was to dig up a recently deceased person and sell the corpse for dissection or anatomy lectures at medical schools. Tuscarawas County was not immune to the practice.

John Louis Roll (1839–1881) was born in Switzerland and immigrated to the United States as a young man, though not much is known of his childhood or parentage. He had arrived in New Philadelphia, Ohio, by the early 1860s and established himself as a "news merchant" in the city and partnered with one of the county's established families, the Fribleys. John married Daniel Fribley's (1812–1904) daughter Cornelia Fribley (1844–1917) in May 1865, and the couple initially set up housekeeping on South Broadway.

John Roll's business did well, and at one point, he partnered with the local newspaper to service subscribers of the paper and make sure that they received their paper in a timely manner. John and Cornelia began raising a family, having two children by 1870, and John became a respected member of the local Masonic Lodge. During the 1870s, John and Cornelia made the decision to relocate to the town of Galion, Ohio, in Crawford County. The family, numbering five children now, relocated but kept close contact with John's professional contacts and Cornelia's family in New Philadelphia.

Photograph of John Roll's headstone and grave in the Fair Street Cemetery, New Philadelphia, Ohio, 2024. *Photo by author.*

The family purchased a home on Orange Street in Galion, and John Roll opened his new business in town. John was a competent businessman and a thoughtful father and husband. Evidence of this is found in the fact that, shortly after he and Cornelia began having children, John wrote out his last will and testament to ensure for the care of his wife and children after his death. Additionally, he took out a $10,000 (equivalent to almost $250,000 today) life insurance policy to be paid to Cornelia in the event of his death.

That untimely death occurred on January 8, 1881, at the age of forty-one, after John became ill with pneumonia and was bedridden for nine days. Cornelia's family arranged for his body to be transported back to New Philadelphia for burial. John's family, and his coffin, arrived in New Philadelphia on Monday, January 10, 1881. John was buried that same day, with the local Masonic Lodge officiating and crowds of mourners at the Fair Street Cemetery. Cornelia and the children, immediately following the funeral, moved into the home of her father, Daniel Fribley.

The Friday after John's burial, Fair Street Cemetery's Sexton John Knisely (1847–1927) discovered that Roll's grave had been tampered with.

It had snowed the evening before, and footprints and drag marks were visible all around the grave. Knisely notified the family and friends, and they immediately investigated the grave by digging down to the coffin. They found that John's coffin had been broken open and his body removed. Another nearby grave had also been tampered with, but the inclemency of the weather must have prevented them from finishing the job. The snowfall that had occurred during the grave robbery enabled the investigators to follow the tracks of the perpetrators all the way to Beaver Dam Road.

As the family and friends searched for more evidence over the weekend, they learned that the night of the body snatching a local young man had purchased a large shipping box from a New Philadelphia merchant. They further learned that the young man had that box, and its contents, shipped via the CTV&W Railroad to Cleveland the day after the grave robbing. That young man was John Heafner (1856–?) of Warren Township, and he had not acted alone.

The identification of John Heafner as one of those responsible for the removal of John Roll from his grave was a significant break in the case. Heafner, originally from Carroll County, had been living and working in Warren Township since at least 1870. Heafner married Clara C. Aldridge (1858–1929) around 1873, and the couple were raising two children by the time John unwisely took part in stealing John Roll's corpse.

Under questioning from authorities, Heafner revealed the names of three others who were involved in the affair. All three of the young men were studying to be physicians in Cleveland, and two of them were Tuscarawas County natives from well-established families. Their names were William Leggett (1854–1888), William Aldridge (1854–c.1884) and one that Heafner only knew as "Dr. Young." Aldridge and Leggett had been neighbors of the Heafners in Warren Township, and Aldridge was also Heafner's brother-in-law.

William Leggett was the son of a prominent Warren Township farmer and Tuscarawas County pioneer named William Leggett (1818–1878). The younger William had been studying medicine with a distinguished local practitioner named Dr. Ezekiel P. Buell (1816–1881) and, at the beginning of 1881, was enrolled as a medical student at the University of Wooster's Medical Department located in Cleveland. Leggett married Mary Baxter (1858–1954) in 1877, and at the time of the grave robbery, the couple had a young son.

The other local perpetrator was William Aldridge, son of Dr. Nicholas Aldridge (1816–1862) of Union Township. William Aldridge was studying medicine with the local physician Dr. John Hill (1833–1904) while also enrolled in the same class as Leggett at the University of Wooster's Medical Department. Aldridge was single, and when he was not in Cleveland, he lived in the household of his widowed mother, Ann Aldridge (1819–1884), in Warren Township.

The identity of "Dr. Young" is harder to determine, though there are hints that lead to two individuals. There were two men named Young listed on the University of Wooster Medical Department's list of students in 1881: a Stark County native senior named Franklin E. Young (1852–1917), who was already practicing medicine, and a junior named Edwin C. Young (?–?). I have been unable to confirm any details about Edwin C. Young beyond the fact that he was a classmate of Leggett and Aldridge. Given that Heafner referred to the third man as "Dr. Young," it is likely that it was the former, as he was practicing at the time.

Following the detention and questioning of John Heafner and his identification of the other three men involved, warrants were issued for their arrest. William Campbell (1834–1886), keeper of the Exchange Hotel in New Philadelphia and a friend of John Roll, boarded a train for Cleveland intending to investigate and recover the body of his friend. When he arrived in Cleveland, he would discover that there were more men, important men, who played a part in the snatching of John Roll.

William Campbell was determined to recover the body of his friend and traveled, along with Enoch Fribley (1846–1913) and Albert Bates Jr. (1852–1934), to Cleveland the Sunday following the body snatching. Fribley was a cousin of John Roll's wife and had been Roll's business partner in New Philadelphia. The three men had determined, with suspect John Heafner's assistance, that the body had been shipped to a Cleveland druggist named William H. Hartness (1836–1912).

William Hartness was born in Stark County, the son of a fairly successful window sash maker in Massillon. He traveled to the West Coast before the Civil War where he worked as a clerk in the city of Portland, Oregon. He returned to Ohio around 1864 and settled in Cleveland, married a local girl and went into business as a druggist. Hartness partnered with a man named Bruce Huling (1841–1881) and opened the druggist firm Hartness & Huling on the public square. That partnership dissolved, and in 1878, the firm was known as W.H. Hartness & Company.

The New Philadelphians, on arriving in Cleveland Sunday afternoon, sought out William Hartness to question him about the delivery of the shipping crate to his establishment. Hartness admitted that he had been the recipient, but when asked about the body, he refused to disclose what the contents of the box had been and what he had done with them. He did, however, inform Campbell that, if no charges were brought in the case, those contents could likely be returned. The search party then went to the Cleveland police and were told by them to wait until Monday to continue the investigation.

Monday morning, three Cleveland police detectives joined the New Philadelphians, and they continued their search for the body of John Roll. One of the detectives traveled to the W.H. Hartness & Company location on the south side of the public square and searched the building from top to bottom. Not surprisingly, given the visit from Campbell the afternoon before, he was unable to locate anything connecting the establishment to the snatching of John Roll, not even the shipping crate Hartness admitted to receiving was found.

The investigation of William Hartness's connection to the case went cold, and the investigation moved on to the possible recipients of John Roll's corpse. The detectives determined to visit three teaching hospitals then operating in Cleveland to discover if any of them had been the recipients of the crate containing the body of John Roll. The medical schools were described in the record by the streets on which they resided: Erie (Cleveland Medical College), Brownell (College of Wooster) and Prospect (Homeopathic Hospital College).

William Campbell decided to return to New Philadelphia early Monday afternoon, January 17, 1881, to provide an update on the search to the family, friends and the press. Campbell informed everyone of his interaction with Hartness and claimed that the police had been less than helpful. He immediately returned to Cleveland that evening and learned what had transpired in the investigation of the three medical colleges during his brief absence.

There were three medical colleges operating in Cleveland in 1881, and all three of them offered classwork on dissection and anatomy. These courses required access to cadavers with which to educate future doctors and provide them "hands-on" learning. Detectives from the Cleveland Police Department and John Roll's friends paid each of these colleges a visit in the search for his corpse.

The detectives visited the Cleveland Medical College, Homeopathic Hospital College and the school of the grave robbers themselves, College of Wooster Medical Department. While the investigators were touring the colleges, only the students at the Wooster Medical Department treated them poorly. There the students followed them around as they investigated, hissed and threatened them with foul language. It was at the Wooster Medical Department that they also found an empty shipping crate, identical to the one that shipped John Roll, addressed to the W.H. Hartness & Company.

Three of the grave robbers were students at the College of Wooster Medical Department, and since the detectives found the suspicious crate on that campus they decided to speak to the college's dean. The dean of the College of Wooster Medical Department, and also the instructor of anatomy at the college, was Dr. Henry W. Kitchen (1843–1907). Kitchen was born in Stark County, Ohio, and had enlisted in the Nineteenth Ohio Infantry at the outbreak of the Civil War. He was wounded at the Battle of Chickamauga, taken prisoner and spent fourteen months in Libby and Andersonville Prisons. After the war, he studied medicine at the University of Michigan and the College of Wooster.

Kitchen was a well-respected member of the medical, and civic, community, as evidenced by his election to various civic positions in the city of Cleveland and county of Cuyahoga. That the detectives chose to interview such a prominent man about a grave robbing indicated that they must have believed they were on the right track. Their willingness to question the man who was a past health officer for the City of Cleveland paid off.

Dr. Kitchen, when asked about the use of cadavers, informed the detectives that the supply of corpses was usually from paupers' graves or from those who had made a point to leave their body to medical science. When questioned about the W.H. Hartness & Company crate on campus, Kitchen explained that it had contained a body recently shipped from Connecticut. The detective, apparently sensing some deception from Dr. Kitchen, then threatened to arrest the three student grave robbers based on the evidence already in hand.

The threat to arrest Aldridge, Leggett and Young was apparently enough to convince Dr. Kitchen to cooperate. The doctor claimed that the theft of John Roll's corpse was totally "unauthorized" and that it was the students' ambition to study anatomy that had led to them digging him up. After learning that the New Philadelphia party was more interested in retrieving John Roll's corpse than in pursuing criminal charges, Dr. Kitchen made an offer. If there would be no arrests made of any of those involved in the snatching of John Roll's corpse, he promised to do everything in his power to help them "regain possession." William Campbell and the others agreed.

Dr. Kitchen informed the party that they could recover John Roll's body at the city morgue, where it would be left, the next day at ten o'clock in the morning. The New Philadelphians did exactly that, and at noon on Tuesday, January 18, they arrived in New Philadelphia with John Roll's remains. He was put to rest, finally, that afternoon.

After finally burying her husband, Cornelia Roll and her children moved into the household of her father. She would never remarry and cared for her father, Daniel Fribley, right up until his death in 1904. Cornelia died in 1917 and is buried next to her husband in Fair Street Cemetery.

It is not entirely clear what happened to John Heafner following the events of January 1881. The record does not indicate that he was ever prosecuted for his role in aiding in the transportation of John Roll's corpse. It should be pointed out that he was not included in the deal to not prosecute made between Dr. Henry W. Kitchen and William Campbell. Heafner does appear in some later newspaper accounts, but only in the transfer of real estate.

Dr. Ezekial P. Buell, who helped educate William Aldridge, died later in the year of John Roll's grave robbing. William Leggett's educator, Dr. John Hill, moved to Indiana and continued to practice medicine until his death in 1904. How much did these two well-respected local doctors know about their students' activities? Had they robbed graves themselves in the past?

Whether William Aldridge completed his medical education is unclear, but it hardly matters, as he died in 1884, only a few years after playing his part in the crime. His classmate William Leggett did complete his education and go on to be a respected physician in his own right, though he would also die within a decade of the crime. The other grave robber, Franklin Young, practiced medicine in Stark County until his death in 1917. Did any of their patients know about their grave robbing past?

The man who dealt in corpses, William Hartness, closed his druggist business in Cleveland shortly after the John Roll incident. He returned to the West for a period, leaving his wife and children comfortably back in Cleveland. He did not return to Cleveland until around 1900. Hartness died in Cleveland in 1912. How many corpses had Hartness trafficked in during the years he operated his drugstore on a busy corner on the Public Square?

The man who purchased the corpse from Hartness, Dr. H.W. Kitchen, suffered very little from his role in the John Roll affair. He continued as one of the prominent medical practitioners and educators of Ohio and served as president of the Cleveland Board of Health and surgeon of the Cleveland Grays. He was elected clerk of the court of common pleas in 1882 and served two terms. Later he became president of the State Banking & Trust Company of Cleveland and played an active role in its management. Dr. Kitchen served as chairman of the Republican Committee of Cleveland, played a prominent role in the Masonic Lodge and was a member of the Cleveland Chamber of Commerce and a number of professional associations, clubs and the Grand Army of the Republic. Dr. Kitchen died in 1907. How many corpses, robbed from their graves by his students, did he purchase for his anatomy classes?

The day that the paper carried the story about John Roll's grave robbing, another article, right next to the Roll story, detailed another botched body snatching. Christina Huffman, recently deceased at the age of sixty, was buried in Carroll County's Mt. Tabor Cemetery on January 4, 1881. Two men dug up her corpse, loaded it into a sleigh and headed west into Tuscarawas County. Tracked by a local sheriff shortly after, the pair were forced to dump Huffman's body on the side of the road in order to make their escape. Had Aldridge and Leggett been responsible for this grave robbing as well? How many graves in Tuscarawas County from the 1800s lie empty because of the practice? We'll never know.

1884

TUSCARAWAS COUNTY'S WILLIAM WATSON'S CALIFORNIA TRAGEDY

Nancy Watson (1832–1910) and a delegation of pallbearers from the Ex-Soldiers and Sailors Association of Newcomerstown were at the railroad station on the morning of Monday, July 14, 1884, to receive the remains of her brother William Watson (1842–1884). William had been killed while mining gold in northeastern California a little less than a month earlier. The pallbearers escorted William's coffin to Nancy's residence, where the funeral was held, and afterward to the Taylor Cemetery near Bakersville, Coshocton County, for burial.

Nancy and William were the children of Irish immigrant Robert Watson (1790–1877) and his wife, Agnes "Nancy" Mance (1796–1874), who had arrived in Adams Township, Coshocton County, Ohio, via Pennsylvania, sometime after 1842. The Watson farm was located just south of the town of Bakersville, about a mile from the Tuscarawas–Coshocton County Line. Robert and Nancy Watson had six children—four daughters and two sons—living on the farm with them in 1850, and William Watson was the youngest.

William attended school near the Watson home during his youth, and when the American Civil War began in 1861, he enlisted for three years in Company K, Twenty-Fourth Regiment, Ohio Volunteer Infantry. The regiment saw service in West Virginia, Tennessee, Kentucky, Mississippi and Georgia until it was mustered out of service in 1864. After his service, William returned home to Ohio and married Teresa Scott (1845–1923) in the spring of 1867. Perhaps it was William's service that motivated his desire to leave Ohio, but shortly after his marriage, he and Teresa moved to Marshall County, Iowa, where their son Robert Watson (1868–1939) was born in 1868.

Gold had been mined and extracted in Tuolumne County, California, since the gold rush of 1849, but improvements in techniques and technology led to a second rush that began around 1880. The Watson family was one of the many families to make the trek and try their hand at finding gold in the area around Sonora, California, called Brown's Flat. They arrived there sometime before the 1880 census was taken in June of that year. The Watsons, after their arrival, were competing with miners who had been in the area since the 1850s.

The kind of gold mining that William Watson used was a method called "placer mining." Placer mining was a method that used moving water to separate gold ore from the surrounding sediment. The most recognizable method was the use of swirling water in a pan, but by 1880, placer mining used flumes of water instead of a small pan. Naturally, this method required a miner to have access to, and move, water from one place to another. It was this need for water that led to conflict between the newcomer Watson and one of the established neighboring miners.

After arriving in California, William enlisted the help of Edmund Gallagher (1863–1907), the son of a longtime Brown's Flat miner, to help in his mining endeavor. William needed to run a pipe of water to his claim in June 1884 but, in order to do so, also needed to cross the property of an adjacent quartz miner named Otis Greenwood (1860–1910). Otis had refused William Watson's previous requests to run the pipe, but that was not going to stop Watson and Gallagher from trying. William and Edmund armed themselves and, with William's young son Robert, began laying the pipe across the Greenwood claim on the morning of June 19, 1884.

Otis Greenwood, armed and accompanied by his armed mother, came down to the location where William Watson was laying the pipe. Otis confronted the men and told him he was going to dismantle the pipe. According to one newspaper account of the altercation, William responded, "The first [expletive] that touches that pipe I will kill him!" Greenwood bent down to move the pipe, and Gallagher brought his shotgun to his shoulder. The gun went off, whether intentionally or not is unknown, and the shot grazed Greenwood. Greenwood then fired his pistol at Gallagher, hitting his hand and grazing his forehead. The second shot from Gallagher's shotgun then hit Otis's mother square in the chest, and she dropped to the ground.

William, Edmund and Robert then started to run when Greenwood fired at William Watson. Watson was wounded and fell to the ground in a nearby ditch as Edmund and Robert made their escape. Greenwood, now realizing that his mother was dead from her wound, walked over to where Watson lay in the ditch. He then fired one shot directly into William Watson's temple, killing him. After the altercation, Otis Greenwood and Edmund Gallagher both turned themselves in to local law enforcement. Following an inquest into what happened at Brown's Flat—and initial charges of murder against Edmund Gallagher—neither Greenwood nor Gallagher was convicted of a crime.

William Watson's body was sent to San Francisco to be embalmed before it was sent, via train, for the long return trip to Newcomerstown for burial in the family plots just south of the Watson property in Adams Township, Coshocton County. Teresa Watson and her son Robert, continuing to mine their claim, lived in Tuolumne County for the remainder of their lives. Robert married very late in life, after the death of his mother, and had no children of his own. The lure of gold had brought William Watson to California, and it was, ultimately, the cause of his posthumous return to Ohio.

1890
THE CHRISTMAS MURDER OF JAMES BOOTH

Our modern conception of the celebration of the Christmas season often involves large family gatherings, community activities, church functions and many other traditions that may be specific to our own families. When James Booth, William Gribble and Henry Wehrli gathered for Christmas 1890, it was under very different circumstances. The holiday would end with one of them dead.

James Booth (b. 1855) was the son of the late John Booth, who was one of Tuscarawas County's largest landholders during his lifetime. The Booths' land was mostly situated in the very southern part of Oxford Township, near the crossroads known as Post Boy Station and east of it (an area today known as Booth).

John Booth's father arrived in Tuscarawas County in the summer of 1811 from England, settling in Oxford Township. John was the middle child in a family of ten siblings, not all of whom lived to adulthood. The family name became common in southern Tuscarawas County. John Booth's wife, Nancy, passed away a few years earlier, and John himself died only two months before the fateful events of Christmas 1890.

Following his father's death, James Booth was living on the family farm with his mother's elderly sister, Mary, Mary's invalid sister and a niece named Alice. The family's young farmhand, William Gribble, was often around but did not live on the farm. Henry Wehrli, a general laborer by trade, had been boarding on the Booth property for a few years by 1890. Henry and James, of similar ages and with a shared interest in alcohol, were reportedly good friends when sober.

William Gribble, the Booths' farmhand, was born in November 1875 and was the son of Peter and Catherine Gribble. William's father was also a general farm and mine laborer in Tuscarawas County during the period. William, not surprisingly, would hang around with James and Henry when they were all on the farm. It would prove to be an unfortunate habit.

Henry Wehrli, the Booths' boarder, was born around 1858 in Switzerland and arrived in the United States in the spring of 1884. During his youth, Henry had attended school until he was thirteen or fourteen; afterward, he worked in a store for a number of years before immigrating to the United States. This story seems to match the arrival document of a twenty-five-year-old Henry Wehrli who arrived in the spring of 1884 through the Port of Boston. He listed his occupation at that time as a grocer. Upon his eventual settling in Tuscarawas County and his boarding at the Booth farm, Henry started working as a miner in the nearby Black Band Ore Mine.

Henry Wehrli purchased six quart bottles of Childs & Co. Rye Whiskey the day before Christmas Eve, and he and James Booth started emptying them right away. By all accounts, both at the time and later, Henry Wehrli and James Booth were the best of friends—when sober. Once they went on what was described as a "spree," then all bets were off, and the two would frequently argue. Henry began his drinking on Tuesday evening, though apparently not enough for the two to become quarrelsome or to prevent Henry from getting to work the next day, Christmas Eve morning. After arriving back at the Booth residence after work, around three o'clock, Henry got together with James and William Gribble, and the real celebrations began. By six o'clock, both James and Henry were "tight" and had already begun to argue and have words. To add insult to injury, Henry was starting to get stingy with the whiskey, further irritating his friend James.

After supper, and given Henry's stinginess with the whiskey, James decided to go to Post Boy Station to pick up some oysters and more whiskey. William accompanied James while Henry stayed back at the house. The two returned around nine o'clock, and the three prepared and ate the oysters in Henry's room. Not surprisingly, Henry and James continued to argue, culminating in Henry accusing James of having stolen a bottle of his whiskey. Tempers were high, and Henry allegedly threatened to kill James. How serious was Henry's threat to James? James apparently thought the threat was very real and locked himself in his room. Henry continued to yell at James through the door but made it clear he would not break the door down, as that would be a "penitentiary offense to break open a locked door." James threatened that if Henry did break the door down, James would "smash his head with a bed slat." This ended the evening, with the two each going to their rooms and William staying in Henry's room after being kicked out of James's.

How much longer the individual drinking continued after the party separated is hard to determine, but at least in James's case, he was up until one o'clock in the morning (Christmas morning). James left the house and went to a neighbor's, where he first asked to be allowed to stay because he was afraid that Henry would kill him. When the neighbor told James to go home and go to bed, James asked him if he had any whiskey he could spare. Turned away by his neighbor, James went back to the house around two o'clock, woke his aunt and told her also that he feared Henry would kill him. She convinced James that he was fine and persuaded him to finally go to bed.

James Booth's Aunt Mary Hart (his mother's sister) awoke at five o'clock on Christmas morning and began to prepare breakfast for her nephew and the other boarders. James woke up shortly after and went to the kitchen, still drunk, and whether he slept at all that night is unknown. An hour later, breakfast was just about ready, and Mary asked James to go wake Henry and William and let them know. James went to Henry's door and kicked it forcefully and yelled to Henry and William that breakfast was ready. Henry angrily replied that if James did not go away he would shoot him. James decided to give the door one more kick and then ran.

Henry was apparently not kidding. As James ran down the stairs, Henry picked up and loaded his single-barrel shotgun and aimed it out the hall window at James as he ran across the yard to the main house. Henry fired once in James's direction but missed him as he went around the corner of the house. This gunshot was heard by a neighbor but, oddly enough, not by Mary in the main house. James picked up two rocks as he ran into the house, apparently to be used to protect himself from Henry, but his aunt told him to throw them away.

Henry, still in a rage and also still drunk, proceeded to put on his clothes and reload his shotgun. In the meantime, James sat down at the dining room table to eat his breakfast, and as Mary poured him a cup of coffee, Henry burst into the room. "For God's sake, Henry, don't shoot him," Mary was reported to have said.

Henry's drunken state got the best of him, however, and from less than ten feet away, he fired directly at James's head. The blast tore into the right side of James's skull at his temple and just above the ear, creating a wound that was described as large enough to put one's fist in. William Gribble, having heard the gunfire, ran into the dining room. There he discovered James, who had fallen off his chair and slumped on the dining room floor, dead. William ran up to his room to get dressed and found Henry there. Informing William that he had killed James, Henry said, "Bring me a revolver and I will kill myself and that will end it." William then watched Henry stuff twenty dollars in his pocket, grab some more shells for the shotgun and snatch, of course, a bottle of whiskey.

William left the room and ran to the barn to get a horse so he could alert someone of what had happened. As he came out of the barn, he ran into Henry again. Henry, with the gun over his shoulder and a bottle of whiskey in his hand, called out and ran off across the field and into the woods to the south.

"Goodbye, Billy!" Henry Wehrli shouted to Booth farmhand and fellow Christmas Eve reveler William Gribble as he headed off to the tree line to the south of the Booth property. Henry made his way south to Cambridge, Ohio, possibly following the tracks of the Cleveland & Marietta Railroad that ran directly from Post Boy Station to Cambridge. Unfortunately for Henry, the news of what had occurred on the Booth farm, and of a $500 reward for his capture, had also reached Cambridge. While en route to Cambridge, Henry tried to alter his appearance by shaving off his mustache and purchasing a new overcoat and hat.

Henry apparently purchased a ticket for a westbound train, its destination unknown. While Henry waited for his train on Tuesday, December 30, 1890, in the station in the Depot Hotel in Cambridge, he was recognized in spite of his effort at disguise. The man who recognized him was a fellow miner named, oddly enough, John Minor of Newcomerstown. Minor solicited the help of a Cleveland & Marietta Railroad employee named Robert Gitkill to detain Wehrli.

Henry was taken to Mayor James Barr of Cambridge, where he was recorded as appearing "very cool" and would say only that he was not guilty. Cambridge's marshal, William Wilkin, was tasked, along with Henry's original captors, with transporting Henry to the jail in New Philadelphia. According to one press account of the journey, the party was greeted by a mob of citizens who were said to have briefly considered lynching Henry right on the spot. Arriving in New Philadelphia, Henry was brought before Mayor MacGregor, and after entering an initial plea of not guilty, Henry was placed in the county jail until a preliminary hearing could be held the following week.

Henry was brought to the courthouse at 1:00 p.m. on Tuesday, January 6, 1891, for a preliminary hearing in front of Mayor MacGregor. Not surprisingly, a large crowd had gathered at the courthouse that day to witness an event not commonly seen in New Philadelphia. Henry, handcuffed to city policeman Dan Sweaney and flanked by his attorneys James O'Donnell and P.H. Olmstead, was presented to Mayor MacGregor on the bench. The mayor then read to the court the names of twenty-six witnesses whose preliminary testimony would be heard that day under questioning by the county prosecutor.

The first witness to testify was, not surprisingly, thirteen-year-old William Gribble, who spent Christmas Eve with Henry and James Booth. He testified that he knew both men and knew them to be "rather mean when drunk." He claimed that he could not tell if either of them was drunk at the time of the murder itself. According to William, he heard James kick the bedroom door in the morning and yell, "Come to breakfast," to William and Henry. William reported that Henry responded to James by yelling, "Go away from that door or I will shoot you!" William then testified that James kicked the door again and then ran down the steps.

The next thing that William reported seeing was Henry Wehrli getting up, grabbing his shotgun, running to the hall window and firing out the window. William assumed Henry had fired at James but could not confirm that he had seen James in the yard below. Henry, according to William, then got dressed, reloaded his shotgun and headed downstairs.

William reported hearing another gunshot, and as he made his way down the stairs, he ran into Henry running up the steps, still carrying his shotgun. William stated that when he reached the dining room, he saw James positioned on his knees, with his head slightly tilted to his left. William mimicked the position in order to show the mayor how he found James. William then laid James down on the floor and could see a large hole in James's head where he had been shot.

William testified that he went back upstairs to Henry's room, where he found Henry and told him, "You have killed Jim." He stated that Henry's response to William was, "Give me a revolver and I will kill myself and that will be the end of it." William stated that Henry then took some money, the shotgun and ammunition and a bottle of whiskey from the room. William left Henry to go back and check on James again in the dining room before Henry reappeared and asked William to "give me a little time to start" before reporting the killing.

Under cross-examination by Henry's attorney, William stated that Henry and James were "good friends when sober but quarreled when drunk." William testified that the two men had been drinking for "several days" before the killing and that he was frightened of James. When asked who killed James Booth on Christmas morning 1890, William Gribble stated it was Henry Wehrli.

James Booth's elderly aunt, Mary Hart, and her invalid sister resided with him on the farm of her late brother-in-law and the victim's father, John Booth. Apparently, her role was to keep house, cook and take care of her nephew and any other boarders and farmhands. She was the only other person present at the time of the murder. Mary Hart testified that she had lived on the farm with her brother-in-law John Booth for a number of years and that James also lived there. Mary did not address James's penchant for drinking other than to state that he "was desperate when drunk." Mary stated that Henry Wehrli had boarded at the home for the past five years and that James had been living on the farm throughout Henry's residency there.

Mary reported hearing a lot of loud talk from the upstairs bedrooms where Henry, James and William Gribble were drinking on Christmas Eve. She did not bother to go upstairs, as she wanted to "let the boys have their time." Regardless, she thought nothing of the noise, as it was apparently common when the men got together and drank. At one point in the evening, likely when James left to look for more whiskey, Mary reported that James came into her room and told her he was going out.

The next day, Christmas morning, Mary heard James making noise upstairs and told him breakfast was ready and to come downstairs to eat. She observed that James was still drunk that morning when he came to eat in the dining room. Mary testified that shortly after James sat down to eat his breakfast, Henry came downstairs with a gun and "looked as though he was going to shoot." As Henry leveled the shotgun at James from about ten feet away, she called out, "Henry, for God's sake don't shoot!"

Newspaper illustration of murderer Henry Wehrli, 1893. *From the* Ohio Democrat *newspaper, New Philadelphia, Ohio.*

Mary said that she immediately ran from the dining room to the room where her sister was and was not present when Henry allegedly pulled the trigger and shot James. She stated that within a few minutes, William came into her room and stated that

James had been shot. The two of them went into the dining room, where Mary said she saw James lying on the floor. William told her that he had laid James down after discovering his body.

Mary stated that they then contacted Dr. Goudy of Newcomerstown to come to the house and that, following the removal of James's body, neighborhood men named Jim Crosley and Dave Daily cleaned up the blood and brain matter in the dining room. Under cross-examination by Henry's attorney, Mary's testimony ended with the observations that James had been carrying a brick or rock in his hand for self-defense and that she hoped that by feeding James breakfast she would "cool his anger."

Four more witnesses, none of whom witnessed the murder itself, provided testimony in the preliminary hearing. The first of those was a neighbor and relative of Mary Hart's named James Hart. Hart noted that he knew both James Booth and Henry Wehrli and that Booth had borrowed a horse from Hart on Christmas Eve in his search for more whiskey. Hart went to the Booth house on Christmas morning to retrieve his horse and stated that he heard loud talk coming from the house. He witnessed James Booth run out of the house at the moment that Henry allegedly shot at him from the window.

Hart testified that he went home after retrieving the horse only to have William Gribble come to his home about half an hour later to tell him that James Booth had been shot. He returned to the Booth house and saw "Jim lying on [the] hearth in a pool of blood and brains scattered about."

The next two witnesses, Peter Gribble and William People, testified to conversations they had with Henry Wehrli regarding James Booth. Peter Gribble, William's father, testified that he had known James Booth for several years and that James was "pretty rough when drinking." He claimed that Henry Wehrli had told him, at least twice, that if James called him "mean names again he would blow his heart out." William People, a miner who worked with Henry Wehrli, testified that on one occasion Henry told him and four other miners that if James Booth ever came into his room and "called him a son of a bitch" that Henry would shoot James.

Dr. John Goudy from Newcomerstown testified that he arrived at the house between 9:00 a.m. and 10:00 a.m. to examine the body. He stated that James's gunshot wound started over his eye and extended backward across his head. Dr. Goudy said that he found wadding and shot inside James's skull, but he had not kept it. Interestingly, Dr. Goudy stated that the wound would be fatal but that he could not state definitively that it killed

James, claiming that it could have been "heart trouble, died from fright, or a hundred other things."

Following the witness testimonies, Henry Wehrli's attorney made the argument to the court that the accused should be charged with homicide since, he argued, Henry did not shoot James with the intent to kill him. The prosecutor, on the other hand, argued for the charge of premeditated murder, claiming that Henry's earlier threats constituted intent. In the end, after reviewing the testimony and evidence, Henry Wehrli was charged with murder and sent to the Tuscarawas County Jail to await his trial date.

Wehrli's defense team consisted of two attorneys, Philip S. Olmstead and James T. O'Donnell, both of whom were well-known Tuscarawas county lawyers by the 1890s. They were of similar age, had both studied law in the offices of local attorneys and socialized with each other, as well as with other lawyers in the county.

Olmstead was the son of Swiss immigrants Jacob and Susan Olmstead of Wayne Township, Tuscarawas County. Philip's parents immigrated from Switzerland to Ohio sometime before 1841 and started a large family. Philip was born on December 6, 1854, one of at least ten children in the Olmstead household. Philip eventually found himself reading law with New Philadelphia attorney J.H. Barnhill in the 1870s. Philip married Cora Gilmore in the fall of 1877 and by 1879 had established a household on the 300 block of East High Street in New Philadelphia.

In 1879, Philip Olmstead was appointed as a justice of the peace for Goshen Township and, after finishing his reading with Barnhill, entered into law practice himself. He initially went into partnership with fellow attorney W.S. Bailey. Olmstead, along with his various partners throughout the 1880s, took on a variety of both civil and criminal cases. He found himself handling estates, real estate purchases and pretty much anything one might expect from an attorney in a small, rural Ohio county.

Henry Wehrli's other attorney, James T. O'Donnell, was born in Mill Township on November 9, 1849. He was the son of local farmer Thomas and Sarah O'Donnell and, during his childhood, helped out on the family farm. He attended New Hagerstown Academy and eventually assumed the role of schoolteacher for a few years before deciding to study law with local attorney J.C. Hance. James went into partnership with Hance after finishing his legal studies in 1873.

James married Margaret Kilgore in 1878 and, following the election of his partner as a judge to the court of common pleas in the fall of 1881, went into practice for himself and then later with another partner, Edward

M. Bailey. By all accounts, James O'Donnell was a respected, capable and successful attorney.

It would appear that the two were friendly, if not good friends, since during the summer of 1888, James O'Donnell and Philip Olmstead, along with Charles Matthews, took a trip to Europe together to, as the newspaper reported, tour the "ould [*sic*] countries." Given their personal relationship and Philip's Swiss heritage, the pair were a good fit to defend the recent immigrant from Switzerland. In 1891, Henry Wehrli's lawyers would find themselves opposed in court by a formidable Tuscarawas County prosecutor.

The Tuscarawas County prosecuting attorney at the time of Henry Wehrli's trial was the grandson of one of New Philadelphia's founding fathers and the son of a county judge. Prosecuting attorney James Graham Patrick was the third generation to carry the James name. His father and grandfather had both been common pleas judges in Tuscarawas County, as had his Uncle Abraham W. Patrick. James Patrick graduated from the New Philadelphia high school in 1872 and attended Franklin College in New Athens and then Wooster University. He studied law with his father and was admitted to the bar in 1877. James then partnered with his father until his election to the position of prosecuting attorney for Tuscarawas County in 1888.

One of James Patrick's assistants on the prosecution was Alexander L. Neely. He was born in Ohio on February 10, 1828, and arrived in Tuscarawas County from Jefferson County in 1852. Neely subsequently read law with attorney J.C. Hance and was admitted to the bar less than two years later in 1854. Neely was elected as the county's prosecuting attorney in 1864 but served in the position for only one year. In the years before the trial of Henry Wehrli, he had partnered with several different county attorneys and was well known and respected as a lawyer. Neely was respected enough in the community that his name was often floated for political positions and nominations, all of which he would decline in preference of practicing law. By the time of Henry Wehrli's trial, Alexander Neely had been practicing law in Tuscarawas County for over thirty-five years.

Abraham W. Patrick, prosecutor James Patrick's uncle, was born and raised in New Philadelphia. His career began in the family printing business, and then he studied the law with Columbus Delano (who would later become secretary of the interior under President Grant) and W.R. Sapp. Their office was located in Mount Vernon, Ohio, where A.W. Patrick was admitted to the bar in 1855. Shortly after he returned to his hometown in 1857, he was elected prosecuting attorney for the county. Ten years later, in 1866, he was elected as a probate judge, served three years and resumed private practice in 1870. A year later, Patrick was elected to the Ohio State Senate, serving one term in that body before once again returning to private practice. These were the men Henry Wehrli's defense team was up against in his murder trial. All of the attorneys were known to one another, as they socialized together and had practiced law in Tuscarawas County for a number of years.

The following testimony from Henry Wehrli was reported in the Thursday, May 28, 1891 edition of the *New Philadelphia Times* and provided the first opportunity for the public to hear Henry's perspective on what had occurred on Christmas morning 1890.

Henry Wehrli's testimony started with him providing the court with background on his life, his immigration to the United States, his work in the local mines and his relationship with the Booth family prior to the death of James Booth. He then moved on to the two days in question, Christmas Eve and Christmas morning. Henry prefaced his testimony by stating, "James Booth and I were on friendly terms when he was sober and when he was drunk he abused me."

Henry began his testimony about the event by stating that he "went to work at 7 o'clock day before Christmas. I returned to the house at 3 o'clock on account of them not hauling ore, having nothing more to do that day. When I came home I washed....I was upstairs after washing, in Jim Booth's room; he had the only grate; my room was not in condition for [a] fire....Jim came up and was sober. He asked me if I wanted some whiskey. I said no—I had some of my own. I got it at New York; sent money order; had 6 bottles, about a quart in each. I knew if I took a drink of his he would want mine. He opened the trunk, pulled out a quart bottle and began drinking; said he was going to have some anyhow."

It was shortly after that William Gribble, one of the primary witnesses, arrived on the scene. After going outside to chat with a neighbor, "Billy Gribble and I [Henry] went back upstairs to Jim's room and Jim was there and pretty well drunk already." It was around five o'clock in the afternoon on Christmas Eve. The trio then went downstairs to supper, and after, "We went up to Jim's room and I [Henry] was reading and Jim asked if I wanted whiskey, and he said he knew where he could get it and left."

Henry testified that "in about an hour James Booth came up; five minutes later Wm. Gribble came; had oysters and crackers, and cooked the oysters.... He [James] gave me one and he and Gribble each took one." It was shortly after eating that Henry claimed James Booth became more belligerent with him and William Gribble.

The testimony continued when Henry stated that "Jim went back on the bed and said some damned son of a bitch stole his bottle....I told him I did not take it—that I had plenty of my own, and he came up to me and asked me for whiskey; I refused it." After being refused whiskey, James "came up to me and said I had better not take anything out of this house and said he would kick the life out of me." Henry stated that he left the room but that James "called me names to Gribble, and said if I came in there he would burst my head with a bed slat, and I went out in the hall and said if he wanted to kill me he would have to come out of there; that I would not break the door—it was a penitentiary offense."

Eventually, James Booth turned his drunken abuse on William Gribble, who then left James's room to spend the night in Henry's room instead. The following morning, Christmas morning, Henry said that "Jim kicked next morning on [the] door of my room and said to come to breakfast, and he said, 'Let me in.' I asked what for? He said, 'To get some whiskey.' I said I had none, and he said 'Go to hell you God damned son of a bitch,' and went downstairs....I was asleep when he first kicked and awakened me.... He said 'I'll burst your God damned brains,' he gave a kick that I thought would break the door and I got up and got my gun and he ran downstairs."

Henry claimed he wanted to scare James and "went and opened a window and looked out and fired in the air to scare him. The gun was pointed in the direction of the stone wall. Jim Booth was at the corner when the gun went off. Jim had in each hand a river biscuit, or river rock, about the size of my fist....I then heard Jim downstairs pounding and said he would burst my head if I came down there, and that I should leave the house."

Henry "wanted to get out and took my gun down with me; had the gun under my arm; gun pointed down; breech of gun was under my arm; hammer just under the arm; I met Mary Hart coming from the hall into the porch. I went into the porch and then into the dining room and Jim was standing close by the grate." According to Henry, James continued to threaten him, saying, "'You God damned son of a bitch, I will fix you,' and he [James] grabbed the gun and I held to it, and in the struggle the gun went off."

During cross-examination, Henry tried to be even clearer about what had occurred in the Booth dining room. "I had no intention to shoot Jm. Booth at all; it went off in struggling over the gun. I had the gun under my arm; the hammer was under my arm. I took the gun along for I was afraid Jm. Booth would burst my head. I stepped into the dining room and Jim made a dash for me and grabbed the gun and we were then by the table when he had the gun. Can't tell the position the gun was in when it went off. I knew if he got the gun he would shoot me down."

Only two individuals were actually in the dining room when James Booth was fatally shot. James Booth was the son of a well-known Tuscarawas County family, and Henry Wehrli was a recent immigrant to Ohio, a stranger to the community. Only one of those individuals was alive to give an account of what happened. Most of Henry's story was corroborated by the witness testimony of William Gribble and Mary Hart. Unfortunately for the jury, neither of them witnessed what had occurred in the dining room. The testimony concluded, Henry Wehrli's fate was now in the jury's hands.

It was at 2:00 p.m. on Wednesday, May 27, 1891, that the jury in Henry Wehrli's murder trial was given their instructions by Judge Pearce. It took the judge the better part of an hour to explain to the jury what they needed to do and to determine, according to the law. The twelve men then retired to the jury room to begin their deliberations.

The first step for the jury was to determine just how close they were to a verdict already. The first poll of the jury determined that eight members were convinced of Wehrli's guilt of murder in the first degree, two members favored conviction on a charge of second-degree murder, one wanted him convicted of manslaughter and one juror was in favor of acquittal.

Discussion and argument went on until suppertime, after which the jury were permitted to take a walk around town prior to returning to the jury room to continue their deliberations. It was around 9:00 p.m. that the jury conducted another poll to see if they had gotten any closer to a unanimous decision. The vote of the jury was now eleven for conviction in the first degree and one for acquittal. This juror believed that, without a direct eyewitness, a conviction of murder in the first degree would be impossible.

The jury continued their deliberations throughout the night, not resting until they could come to a unanimous decision. At 3:30 a.m. on Thursday, after nearly twelve hours of discussions, the jury informed the judge that they had finally reached a verdict. The court staff and parties were informed that they should convene at 5:00 a.m. to hear the verdict.

The jury had found Henry Wehrli guilty. As the verdict of guilty of murder in the first degree was read, Henry's attorneys requested a poll of the jury. Each of the jurors affirmed their verdict. James Edie, the oldest juror, openly wept as the verdict was read and, according to the newspaper, showed far more emotion than the defendant. After the verdict was read, the defense announced their intention to appeal and request a new trial. Henry Wehrli was transferred to the county jail to await his sentencing.

Henry Wehrli was spared capital punishment, instead being sentenced to life in the Ohio State Penitentiary. However, after ten years—and due to arguments about the fairness of his trial (including from prosecutors like A.W. Patrick)—Wehrli was granted parole in 1902. As part of his parole, he was prohibited from drinking alcohol of any kind. He never married and would eventually settle in Mineral City with his brother and return to the work of mining. Henry Werhli died in 1929 and is buried in East Avenue Cemetery in New Philadelphia.

1893

SHOT IN HER BED: THE EMMA McDONALD KILLING

Harry T. Stewart (1868–1895) was the son of Virginia-born Guernsey County, Ohio farmer James Stewart (1826–1892) and his wife, Rebecca Right (1836–1921). Harry grew up and worked on the family farm in Adams Township, Guernsey County, just outside of the community of Mantua. By the time Harry relocated to the east end of Uhrichsville in the 1890s, he was a flagman for the Panhandle Railroad. It was around this time that Harry made the acquaintance of a young lady named Emma Myers.

There are two women named Emma Myers recorded in the 1880 and 1900 censuses for Tuscarawas County, and based on age and proximity, it is most likely that the Emma Myers (1874–1958) known to Harry was one who lived with her family in the town of Tuscarawas in 1880 and 1900. This Emma would also later live in Uhrichsville after her marriage. At the time that Harry and Emma knew each other, Harry was paying for her to board at the home of George Lyle of Dennison. Whatever romance may have existed between the two had soured by the spring of 1893.

Emma Myers was avoiding Harry in April 1893 when Harry and a friend named John Stanart, on their way back from Lyle's house, where they were looking for her, came upon Emma McDonald (1872–1893), who was boarding at Lyle's as well. This Emma was the stepdaughter of Theophelus Steese (1827–1897) and his wife, Lavinia Castleman McDonald (1845–1927), and was due to be married in less than a week to a man named Orr Davis. According to later newspaper reports, Emma McDonald was assisting Emma Myers in her efforts to steer clear of Harry. Harry asked

Early twentieth-century postcard image of Third Street, Uhrichsville, Ohio. *Tuscarawas County Historical Society.*

Emma McDonald if she had seen Emma Myers, and she told him that she saw Myers cross the tracks on her way home.

After about an hour, Harry was determined to see Emma Myers and borrowed a .32-caliber revolver from his friend. He stated that he would "go into that house if I have to kick the door down." The pair arrived at the Lyle residence around 9:30 p.m. on April 15, 1893, and convinced George Lyle to let them in. They went to the room shared by both Emmas and there woke up Emma McDonald, who was lying in her bed. Harry, brandishing the revolver, asked where Emma Myers was. Emma responded that she did not know, and Harry, likely in an effort to frighten her, snapped the revolver's hammer back. Harry was careless, though, and pulled the trigger, sending a single round through Emma McDonald's arm and into her chest. She was dead in less than ten minutes.

Harry Stewart was quickly arrested, and two months later, a grand jury indicted him for second-degree murder. Harry's friend John Stanart was charged with carrying a concealed weapon and given a twenty-dollar fine. Friends and family members of Harry were able to raise the necessary bond to have Harry released prior to his trial. As the trial date grew closer, Harry was less optimistic about his chances of winning his case in court and wanted to avoid the possibility of a life sentence. Harry's attorney negotiated a plea deal with the court, and Harry pleaded guilty to a charge of manslaughter and was sentenced to ten years in the Ohio State Penitentiary.

Harry Stewart was at the Ohio State Penitentiary for less than a year when he started showing symptoms of tuberculosis. As the prisoner's condition deteriorated, his attorney applied to the Ohio parole board, with support from the prison warden and chaplain, to have Harry released. The parole board, likely as a response to Harry's highly contagious illness as much as to any sense of clemency, agreed, and he was released in January 1895. Harry's health continued to decline throughout that year, and on November 7, he died at his mother's home in Guernsey County. The killer of Emma McDonald outlived his victim by less than three years.

1899
A POISONING ON CROOKED RUN

Members of the Fisher family of Crooked Run were no strangers to being in the newspaper when the story of their poisoning made news in the early fall of 1899. Thirty years earlier, they had been the focus newspaper stories about the possible possession or bewitching of their daughter Mary. That story, thankfully for the family, quietly drifted from the pages of the newspaper to be forgotten. Their latest sensational episode, however, appeared in the local papers, off and on, for almost ten years.

This time the drama surrounded a different daughter of George Fisher (1830–1900), Lilly Fisher (1872–1933), and her husband, William M. Stiers (1864–1954). William Stiers was originally from Guernsey County, Ohio, and, for reasons yet to be determined, was raised by his Uncle Ebenezer Stiers (1832–1907) and his wife, Elizabeth Grayhem (1832–1880). William was in documented trouble with the law a couple of times during his youth: charged for shooting at a woman in 1885 and then for theft in 1892.

There is no record of exactly how, or when, William first met Lilly Fisher, though it must have occurred before October 1895 (for reasons that will soon be apparent). The couple married in Tuscarawas County in early February 1896, though the marriage record includes the words "Do Not Publish" scrawled across the record. Six months later, the couple would welcome their only child, Inez May, in June 1896. Shortly after the birth of her daughter, and for reasons not made public, Lilly left William, and she and Inez moved back into her father's home.

A newspaper account from early February 1896 documents an occurrence where William Stiers allegedly threatened Lilly's father, George, in a menacing manner. The manner is not elaborated on, but it was significant enough to warrant Stiers's arrest and subsequent appearance in court. While in court, Stiers represented himself and wanted to recite a poem he had written that expressed all the ways he claimed he was being wronged by the Fisher family. The newspaper derisively reported that Stiers was "off mentally" and that "Blackstone, poetry and family troubles are too much for one man to carry around."

According to one source, Stiers spent the next couple of years harassing the Fisher family and made at least two attempts to kidnap his daughter, Inez. On one attempt, he managed to grab her from George Fisher's yard, fired shots at the pursuing family and eluded capture for several days by traveling with the girl only at night. He had already been issued a suspended sentence for his previous alleged tormenting of the Fishers, and so, after his eventual capture, he was sentenced to the county workhouse for six months.

During the summer of 1899, George Fisher hired a local carpenter with the surname Kuhns to undertake work on the family's barn. This was likely Dover resident William H. Kuhns (1847–1904) and his father and brother, who were carpenters working in the area at that time. The carpenters were working on the barn during the first week of September when George Fisher and his family invited the men to an afternoon meal. As the meal progressed, William Kuhns became violently ill, and other members of the party began to feel sick as well. They placed Kuhns into a buggy and drove him immediately to a local doctor who, on treating Kuhns and then examining the food eaten, determined that he and the rest of the party had been poisoned.

The doctor concluded that the butter that had been used during the meal was tainted with strychnine, and the Fisher family immediately suspected Stiers of having done the deed. According to the Fishers, Stiers was known to ride a bicycle from his family's home in Kimbolton to the area, and bicycle tracks were found on the road leading to the Fisher farm. William Stiers's alleged and real past behavior toward the family, the family's standing in the community and the circumstantial bicycle trail was enough for local law enforcement to issue a warrant for his immediate arrest.

The Tuscarawas County jury that tried William Stiers did not take long to convict him of the poisoning, and the local judge sentenced William to eight years in the Ohio Penitentiary. Shortly after this conviction, one of his main antagonists, George Fisher, passed away in March 1900. Luckily for Stiers, his friends and neighbors in Guernsey County were able to raise enough money to have his case heard in circuit court several months after his original conviction. After Stiers served six months in jail, the circuit court ruled in June 1900 that the evidence presented in his original trial was not enough to warrant Stiers's conviction. He was released shortly after, but there was no reconciliation with the Fisher family or his wife.

William returned to his uncle's home in Guernsey County and, three years later, petitioned for divorce from Lilly Fisher. William accused Lilly of desertion and both her and her late father of extreme cruelty. He argued that they had conspired to cause his arrest in the poisoning case, essentially accusing them of the crime. William's petition was granted by the courts, and he and Lilly were officially divorced, though she and their daughter continued to use his surname.

Lilly Fisher Stiers never remarried and passed away in 1933. The poisoned carpenter, William Kuhns, died an untimely death in 1904, though whether his death was the result of his poisoning in 1899 is unknown. William Stiers remarried, and for short time, he and his new wife operated a photography studio in Uhrichsville. William's new wife accused him of behaving erratically and violently toward her, and the couple divorced after less than ten years of marriage. William went on to become a licensed chiropractor and, restlessly, moved around quite a bit before settling down in Cadiz in the 1920s. He maintained a relationship with his daughter over the years until his death at the age of ninety in 1954.

1901

UNSOLVED AND FORGOTTEN: THE MURDER OF MRS. MARTHA HENSEL

A particularly grisly murder took place in New Philadelphia, Ohio, in the fall of 1901. Despite the violence of the crime and the fact that there were a number of potential suspects, no one was ever brought to justice. The victim's death and life were subsequently forgotten.

It was a Wednesday afternoon in late October 1901 when two North Third Street (modern Second Street NE) boys grabbed a small bag and headed out to collect walnuts in the woods east of a farmer's field that bordered their street. As they climbed over the fence, one of the boys noticed something in the field about one hundred yards or so away. At first, they thought perhaps someone had gotten drunk and passed out in the recently harvested field of corn and cabbages. The older of the two boys took another look and realized immediately that it was the body of a woman. They ran back to the nearest home and told the occupants what they had seen.

Within a short time, a small crowd had gathered around the body, and neighbors were able to identify the woman as Martha J. Hensel (1853–1901), the widow of Joshua Hensel (1834–1901), who had died from natural causes only a couple of weeks earlier. Martha had been Joshua's third wife, after he divorced one wife and a second had died, and he had been her second husband. She had divorced Zoar tavernkeeper Emanuel Hostetler (1847–1930) in 1893. Joshua had seven children with his first wife, and Martha had two children with Emanuel.

Very little is known about Martha's life before her marriage to Emanuel in 1873. She was born in Indiana, her maiden name was Grant and she met, and married, Emanuel when he was operating a saloon in LaGrange County, Indiana. Emanuel was born in Wayne County, Ohio, and the stay in Indiana was a brief one. He was operating his tavern and restaurant and living in Zoar at least as early as 1884. There is no indication in the record why Emanuel and Martha divorced or why Joshua Hensel and his first wife did either.

Among the authorities to arrive on the scene was the county coroner, whose examination of the body yielded information on just how violent the attack had been. Martha was lying on her back, her open eyes covered in blood and her body surrounded by a thick pool of coagulated blood. The coroner estimated that she had lost nearly three-quarters of the blood in her body and that her murder had likely occurred early the previous evening. He determined that she had been struck on the head several times with a sharp object, either a hammer claw or an axe, and the blows had crushed her skull. The assailant had struck her twice in the back of the head, twice on top and then two more times on her face. It was a particularly brutal—and believed personal—killing.

The authorities searched Martha's person and the field, looking for clues about who had committed this murder and why. Martha was still holding her house and outbuilding keys in her hands, and the money that she had on her, totaling almost fifty dollars and partially concealed, was untouched. The murderer obviously had not searched her after the crime, content with savagely ending her life. There was no murder weapon found in the field or at the Hensel home when it was searched a short time later. The only potential physical clue was a muddy footprint on her apron that may have been left by the murderer.

The lack of physical evidence did not prevent the public, the newspapers and the authorities from speculating about who murdered Martha Hensel and why. The one physical clue, the shoeprint, was said by one paper to be that of a woman's shoe. Whether it was the assailant or Martha's print was not clear. This led that newspaper to suspect that possibly she was killed by a jealous woman, though jealous of what was hazy. Another theory was that, apparently, someone in the neighborhood sent a threatening letter to the person who planned to sell the Hensels their property. That person indicted that they did not want the Hensels living there. The letter writer threatened to burn down the seller's home, which did occur after the sale to the Hensels was complete. Perhaps this person had decided to kill Martha now that Joshua Hensel was out of the picture as well. Another theory put forward by the press was that Mrs. Hensel somehow knew the identity of

West High Street looking east from the Courthouse Square in New Philadelphia, Ohio, 1912. *Tuscarawas County Historical Society*.

a serial arsonist that had been plaguing the city for some time and that the person murdered her to conceal their identity. Though how she would have known that information is never presented.

Unlike the out-of-town newspapers, the New Philadelphia newspaper was more circumspect in its speculation on why Mrs. Hensel was murdered. That did not stop the paper from rumor-mongering about Hensel's character, her divorce and her personality. The paper mentioned that numerous potential perpetrators aligned with those rumors were interviewed by the authorities, adding the appearance that the rumors may have been true. Interestingly, the character of her late husband, Joshua Hensel, a longstanding member of the community and a well-known Civil War veteran, was never in question. Additionally, her ex-husband, Emanuel Hostetler, did not have his character examined in the press. Regardless of the killer's motive and whether any of the rumors were true is irrelevant. Martha Hensel did not deserve what happened to her that October evening.

A couple of days after her murder, her two sons from her previous marriage came to town from Zoar to gather up their mother's belongings from the Hensel home. There was no grand jury investigation into who may have murdered Martha Hensel, just the coroner's inquest to determine cause and method of death. The story of the murder disappeared from the newspapers almost as quickly as it arrived, with no further details on the case surfacing. The sole mention of it came in January 1902 when a woman went missing, only to be found later. The article noted that the town was still on edge from the unsolved murder of Mrs. Hensel.

Despite her divorce, Martha Hensel was buried in the Hostetler plot in Zoarville Cemetery in Zoar, Ohio. Emanuel was buried there with her after his death in 1930. The identity and motive of Martha's murderer, very much like her early life, remain a mystery to this day.

1901
STRIKEBREAKERS AND THE KILLING OF JACK O'NEIL

Alfred G. "Jack" O'Neil (1864–1901) was born in Virginia, though little else is known about his life before his arrival to Ohio sometime in the 1880s. Jack was drawn to Ohio by the growing steel and iron industries and, by the time he married Ohio-born widow Keziah Ann Davault (1853–1932) in 1889, was living and working in Stark County, Ohio. The couple moved into a home on South Avenue in Dover, Ohio, after Jack found work at the Reeves Iron Company, owned at the time by the American Sheet Steel Company.

Newspaper accounts recorded Jack as being "a splendid specimen of physical manhood, weighing possibly 200 pounds with the broad, magnificently developed chest of a prize fighter." While not everyone working in the local steel and iron industry were members of organized labor, Jack was a member of the Amalgamated Association of Iron and Steel Workers, which was founded in 1876. That union, in an attempt to force the American Sheet Steel Company to unionize all their mills, called a strike in July 1901.

The strike dragged on for two months, but the American Sheet Steel Company was resolute in its position to not force unionization on its nonunion mills. It even brought in nonunion strikebreakers from outside Dover in order to operate the unionized mill in Dover. This effort almost led to a full-scale riot in late August 1901, but Tuscarawas County Sheriff Darius Hefling (1836–1915) was able to keep order. The strike ended in mid-September 1901 with no change in the unionization of nonunion mills

Top: Bird's-eye view of Canal Dover, Tuscarawas County, Ohio, 1899. *Library of Congress, Geography and Map Division.*

Bottom: The American Sheet and Tin Plate Company, circa the early twentieth century. *Tuscarawas County Historical Society.*

The Wooster Avenue Bridge looking northeast, Dover, Ohio, circa the early twentieth century. *Tuscarawas County Historical Society*.

of the American Sheet Steel Company, and the unionized workers returned to work.

Even though the strike was over, many of the strikebreakers remained in Dover to work in the mills. Among them were six men who had been relocated during the strike from the American Sheet Steel Company's mill in Westmoreland County, Pennsylvania. Those men—Joseph H. Cricks (1845–1914), his son Henderson W. Cricks (1876–1945), Elliott Klingensmith (1880–1914), Edward B. Lemon (1877–?), Henry Y. Zimmerman (1874–1937) and Herman J. Dixon (1878–1935)—were all boarding in the home of Andrew Godfrey (1848–1940) on Front Street in Dover. The home sat just west of the Wooster Avenue bridge in Dover.

Less than two weeks after the strike ended, Alfred "Jack" O'Neil, his friend and fellow millworker Orin McDowell (1869–1949) and a few other union men were walking to Dover around 9:00 p.m. on September 28, 1901, after visiting the fairgrounds for the day. As they passed the mill, they jokingly tried to drag the mill's young gate guard, Jesse Hiram Dotts (1884–1926), along with them. As they crossed the Wooster Bridge, they saw the six Pennsylvania strikebreakers walking home from the mill. Words were exchanged between the groups, and when the dust cleared, Jack O'Neil lay dead from a gunshot wound in his back and Orin McDowell was wounded.

The six men retreated to their boardinghouse, and several minutes later, it was surrounded by union millworkers and locals. Dover's mayor, English-born John D.T. Bold (1859–1919), called on Sheriff Hefling once again.

Canal Dover Policeman Robert McCluney, circa the early twentieth century. *Tuscarawas County Historical Society*.

Sheriff Hefling took the six men into custody, and on October 4, 1901, all six were indicted for manslaughter. A month later, Tuscarawas County Prosecutor Joseph Greene (1860–1927) decided, because the investigation into who the actual shooter was had been unsuccessful, that it would be too costly to try all six men and dropped the indictments. All six men went free. Alfred "Jack" O'Neil's funeral was one of the largest ever held in Dover at the time; it included over six hundred union workers and the Reeves Military Band and was led by thirty little girls in white dresses and black sashes. Jack O'Neil was buried in Maple Grove Cemetery.

1903
A MURDER IN KLONDIKE

Many immigrants arrived in Tuscarawas County at the turn of the twentieth century to work in the industries that dominated the local economy. Among them were coal miners who came to work the county's numerous coal mines, leading to the creation of company towns like Klondike. Many of the stories of these immigrants, like the company towns they worked in, have been forgotten or overlooked. This is one of those stories.

During the late 1890s, the Beaver Dam Coal Company, based in Cleveland, began to make plans to develop the coal fields in Tuscarawas County's Beaver Dam Valley. The location they selected straddled the Goshen and Union Township line about five miles east of New Philadelphia, Ohio, and was just to the east of Vickers Post Office on the Roxford Road. The company arranged for a branch of the Cleveland & Pittsburgh Railroad to be constructed to the area and laid out a company town to house the miners needed to work the new mine. The town was named Klondike after the popular gold rush region in Alaska, which was reported on in all the newspapers of the day.

The opening of the Beaver Dam mine could not have come at a better time. A large mine operated near Midvale by the Midvale-Goshen Coal Company had recently ceased operation, so many of those miners made their way to the new town of Klondike to find work. The miners were competing for jobs in the new Beaver Dam mine with large numbers of recently arrived immigrants from southern and eastern Europe, among them many Hungarian newcomers. One of those newcomers was John Elek (1859–1926), who had arrived with his family around 1900. In 1903, they were living in one of the company houses along with four other miners.

Two of the men boarding with the Eleks apparently took a shine to their seventeen-year-old daughter, Mary (1887–1965), who could speak English and often helped with preparing the meals. Those two men were Gyorgy Novak (1865–aft. 1913), usually referred to as George Novak, and Mayk Forkass (1875–1903), who was usually referred to as Michael Farkas. Both men had arrived from Hungary within the last two years and made their way to Ohio to work in the Beaver Dam mine. Neither spoke English very well.

The evening of June 27, 1903, the four men boarding at the Eleks' house decided to play cards after dinner. The men went out to the front yard, sat on some benches and began playing. At some point during the card game, Mayk Forkass allegedly made some comments about Mary, and Gyorgy's chances with her, that angered Gyorgy. What Mayk may have not known was that Gyorgy had in his possession a .32-caliber pistol and a willingness to use it. Gyorgy drew the pistol and fired five shots into Mayk, with one striking him in the head, causing a fatal wound. Gyorgy then ran off into the woods south of town.

County law enforcement were notified, and they quickly arrived in Klondike to search for the offender but had no luck finding him. A reward of $400 was offered for anyone who could locate Novak, and many men from the community descended on Klondike to aid in the search. Eventually, the deputy sheriff learned that Novak was returning to town late at night to find food and then absconding back into the woods. The deputy sheriff and another man staked out the town, and three days after the murder, Novak was arrested at midnight on Tuesday, June 30, 1903. Novak was then taken to the Tuscarawas County Jail in New Philadelphia to await justice.

Gyorgy Novak was brought into his arraignment a few days later, and the mayor's court heard testimony, translated by Mary Elek, from a number of people who had witnessed the murder. The mayor determined that Novak was to be held without bail while a grand jury was paneled to look at the case. The grand jury ultimately handed down a charge of first-degree murder on October 31, 1903, to which Novak pleaded not guilty. However, a few days later, after meeting with his attorneys, Novak returned to court and pleaded guilty to second-degree murder. He was then sentenced to life in prison at the Ohio Penitentiary in Columbus.

As Gyorgy Novak sat in a prison cell at the Ohio Penitentiary in Columbus, changes began happening in and around the mining town of Klondike. First, Klondike merged with a neighboring community, and the two became known as the town of Roswell. Second, the Elek family moved from Klondike to Cleveland, Ohio, and Mary Elek, the woman whose affections allegedly triggered the murder, married around 1909. Lastly, in 1910, the Beaver Dam Coal Company abandoned the mine in Klondike, and many of the miners there moved on to new locations and new lives elsewhere in Ohio. Gyorgy Novak was paroled in 1913 after serving only ten years of a life sentence. His life after prison is elusive.

1903
THE UNFORTUNATE DEATH OF MATTHEW COONEY

The day started out as one of celebration by a group of Wainwright coal miners at the arrival of a child but ended in a catastrophe brought on by too much drink and a double-barreled shotgun.

Matthew Cooney (1880–1903) and his wife, Laura Lorenz (1883–1959), married in January 1903 and welcomed their first child on November 4, 1903. The child, a boy, was the motivation for Matthew and his fellow coal miners and friends to celebrate ten days later. The men celebrated in the best way they knew how: by drinking and socializing all day, all night and into the early hours of the next day. They all found themselves at Welsh immigrant William Lewis's (1839–1919) Wainwright home in the early morning hours of November 14, 1903.

Matthew Cooney was born in Summit County, Ohio, in June 1880, the son of Matthew and Elizabeth Cooney. He was working as a coal miner and living in Warwick Township by 1900, when he was recorded as boarding in the home of his future father-in-law, John Lorenz (1846–1905). William Lewis's son Evan Lewis (1880–1953) was one of Matthew's friends and also worked as a coal miner along with his father and brother. The celebrating miners began their festivities in the afternoon and were eventually joined by Evan, who had been drinking at a tavern all day, at the Lewis home.

When Evan Lewis arrived at the home, the men there were drinking, playing the harmonica, singing, dancing and generally having a good time. It was nearly midnight when Matthew Cooney told Evan about a disagreement he had with another miner earlier in the day. Evan wanted Matthew to go

Wainwright, Ohio, circa the early twentieth century. *Tuscarawas County Historical Society.*

down to the man's house and fight him and punctuated his argument by grabbing the family's double-barreled shotgun and telling Matthew to follow him. Evan got seventy-five yards from the home before he realized Matthew had not followed him. Drunkenly firing off one shell into the air, he made his way back to the house.

When he returned, he found Matthew sitting at the kitchen table drinking, a kerosene lamp above his head the only light in the room, and Evan's father passed out under the table. Evan sat down on the opposite side of the table and laid the shotgun down in front of him. Realizing that the shotgun was still loaded and cocked, he went to slowly release the hammer, but it slipped and the shotgun fired its second shell, knocking out the lamplight. In the dark, Evan called out to Matthew but received no answer. He then called out to his father, still no answer. Believing he may have killed one or both of them, Evan ran from the house.

Neighbors and others in the house heard the gunshot and, when they entered the kitchen and lit the light, discovered Matthew Cooney dead in his chair. The top of his head had been completely removed by the shotgun blast, brains and blood scattered on the walls and floor. Under the table, still passed out, was Evan's uninjured father. Evan, meanwhile, was hiding in a coal mine nearby. After he learned of Matthew's death the next day, he turned himself in to the county authorities. He claimed at his preliminary hearing that it was all a horrible accident but was held on the charge of second-degree murder as he awaited his day in court.

The brief trial of Evan Lewis took place in February 1904, and numerous witnesses were called to the stand. Most, if not all, stated that Evan and Matthew were friends, that there had been a great deal of drinking done that day and that there was no animosity between the two men. The jury found Evan Lewis guilty of the lesser charge of manslaughter. Evan was taken to the Ohio State Penitentiary to serve an eight-year sentence but was paroled four years later. He would marry and have some future run-ins with the law but never had any children. Evan Lewis died in 1953.

Matthew Cooney was buried in East Avenue Cemetery in New Philadelphia, though no headstone can be located there for him. His wife went on to remarry and have more children with her later husbands. Matthew's son, whom they were celebrating that fateful night, went on to be a well-respected local architect and executive for the B.F. Goodrich Company in Akron, Ohio. He died in 1960. The events of that night in Wainwright were tragic and separated a new father from his infant son. Matthew Cooney can rest peacefully, though, knowing that his son grew to be a successful and respected member of the community.

1905

SCANDAL IN NEW PHILADELPHIA: THE WHITMIRE-STUDER AFFAIR

In the early twentieth century, Tuscarawas County was not immune from vice, as evidenced by this case from 1905 involving a local couple, a Canton boardinghouse proprietor and two girls from Dennison.

Two teenage girls from Dennison, Ida and Winifred, were arrested at the end of August 1905, charged with prostitution and taken to the Tuscarawas County Jail. While there, and perhaps under questioning by the local authorities, they named the parties who had recruited them into the profession. The girls gave the names of two individuals: Alice Whitmire (1873–1910) of New Philadelphia and Caroline Studer (1857–1918) of Canton, Ohio. Later, Alice's husband, Ulysses (1865–1943), was also named. The three were arrested shortly after and charged with "inducing female persons under the age of 18…to enter a house of prostitution."

Ulysses Whitmire was a coal miner and the son of a coal miner who had lived his whole life in New Philadelphia. Alice, born in Youngstown, Ohio, was the daughter of a New York–born widow who had moved to New Philadelphia around 1873. The couple married in 1891 and, after living first on West High Street, moved into a rented house on West St. Clair Street in New Philadelphia west of the B&O Railroad Station. They were living there with their three children and Ulysses's father when they were arrested in the fall of 1905.

Caroline Studer was born in Switzerland and immigrated to the United States sometime before 1880. She initially married a hotelkeeper in Holmes County, Ohio, before marrying Stark County hotelkeeper

Joseph Studer (1865–1920) in December 1890. Joseph Studer's saloon and boardinghouse, previously known as the United States Hotel, was located directly across from the Pittsburgh, Fort Wayne and Chicago Railway station at the terminus of East Tenth Street in Canton, Ohio. This location would seem to have been the "house of prostitution" mentioned in the indictment of the three.

The relationship between the Whitmires and the Caroline Studer is difficult to ascertain, and how these girls from Dennison were introduced to Caroline is unknown. Later newspaper reporting indicated that the two girls had been offered jobs as waitresses at the Studer saloon in Canton, but who had made that offer is unclear. An examination of the 1900 census record for the Studers' boardinghouse listed a number of young, single men and women as living there with various occupations listed. It certainly appeared that the old United States Hotel was serving (or maybe had long served) as a house of prostitution.

Alice and Ulysses Whitmire were tried separately from Caroline Studer at the Tuscarawas County Courthouse in October 1905. It also should be noted that, while this trial was going on, Caroline's husband, Joseph Studer, was under indictment in Indiana for passing counterfeit money. The local

The Tuscarawas County Courthouse and Square, circa 1905. *Tuscarawas County Historical Society.*

jury acquitted both of the Whitmires after the jury deliberated for just over an hour. Caroline Studer was not as lucky. She was convicted and sentenced to four years' hard labor at the Ohio State Penitentiary. Meanwhile, Ida and Winifred were sent to the Ohio Girls' Industrial School.

Alice Whitmire lived only five more years after the trial, dying from a uterine hemorrhage in December 1910 at the age of forty-seven. Caroline Studer served her sentence at the Ohio State Penitentiary, returned to Canton and died in January 1918 at the age of sixty-five. Joseph Studer died in June 1920 at the age of fifty-seven, outliving his older wife by only two years. Ulysses Whitmire, who went on to operate the Zoar Fish Hatchery, was the last of the principals to die in October 1943 at the age of seventy-six. The location of the Studers' hotel (and brothel) in Canton, Ohio, is now an empty lot.

1900s

THE "BLACK HAND" IN TUSCARAWAS COUNTY

During the early 1900s, the burgeoning Italian immigrant community in Tuscarawas County watched with trepidation as the local newspaper carried stories of the extortion of their fellow countrymen in cities like New York and Pittsburgh by a shadowy group referred to as the "Black Hand Society." It would not be long before the "hand" appeared in their own neighborhoods.

The Black Hand Society traced its roots to eighteenth-century Italy, but its early twentieth-century form was the result small groups of loosely organized criminals targeting their fellow immigrant neighbors. The group was firmly established in the Italian immigrant communities of most major cities in the United States by 1900, and as the Italian immigrant population sought employment in other locations like Tuscarawas County, the small criminal element among them followed as well. These criminals typically targeted the more successful immigrants in their own community, though they were known to threaten anyone. The extortionists' modus operandi was to send a letter to a potential victim threatening them with injury, kidnapping, arson or murder unless a payoff was made. These letters were occasionally decorated with threatening symbols and frequently signed with the image of a black hand.

The *New Philadelphia Democrat and Times* newspaper ran a story on August 25, 1904, about the recovery of a New York City youth believed to have been kidnapped by "members of the Italian Black Hand society." The newspaper did not describe the Black Hand in detail, so one must assume that it believed its readers were already well aware of the group and its activities. This was the first time that the group appeared by name in the Tuscarawas County press, though the local Italian immigrant community had surely heard of the group via word of mouth before 1904.

Over the next four years, more stories of extortion and murder appeared in the local newspapers. Large cities like New York and Pittsburgh were joined by smaller cities like Wheeling, West Virginia, and Wilkes-Barre, Pennsylvania, in reporting crimes undertaken by the Black Hand. Anywhere that Italian immigrants were working and living, they were followed and victimized by Black Hand criminals. Tuscarawas County, with its many coal and clay mines, railroad work and industries providing jobs to Italian immigrants, was about to record its first run-in with the Black Hand Society.

Biagio (William) Bonanno immigrated to the United States in 1898, and following the work and his fellow Italian immigrants, he in time settled down in Dennison, Ohio, and started a small grocery business. Three years later, he had saved enough money to bring his wife, Maria (Mary), to Dennison as well. The couple operated their grocery store at 13 North Third Street, just up from the railroad tracks. In less than ten years of arriving, Biagio Bonanno had successfully established himself as a small business owner in his new, adopted country.

Bonanno opened his mail on Saturday, May 30, 1908, and discovered something dreadful. Among the delivery was an extortion letter from the Black Hand demanding that he pay them $2,000 (close to $50,000 today). The extortionists claimed to know that the Bonannos had saved up over $3,000. The letter instructed Bonanno to travel to Pittsburgh on June 20 and that seven men would be waiting there for him to collect the money. He was told to wrap one hand in a red handkerchief and smoke a cigar so that the men could identify him. Bonanno reported the letter to the local police and told the newspaper that he planned to shutter his grocery store and leave Dennison with his family until it was safe to return.

Whether he ever paid the extortion money is unknown, but less than a year later, agents of the U.S. Postal Inspection Service arrested two Dennison men for mailing Black Hand extortion letters. The men, Antonio Vicario and Augustino Marfisi, were arrested as part of a larger effort that targeted Ohio's Black Hand operatives. Since the men were alleged to have sent the letters via the U.S. mail, they were charged with federal crimes. Only one of the men, Antonio Vicario, was convicted and sentenced to two years at the federal prison in Leavenworth, Kansas. Biagio Bonanno returned to Dennison before 1910 and continued to operate his grocery store until his death.

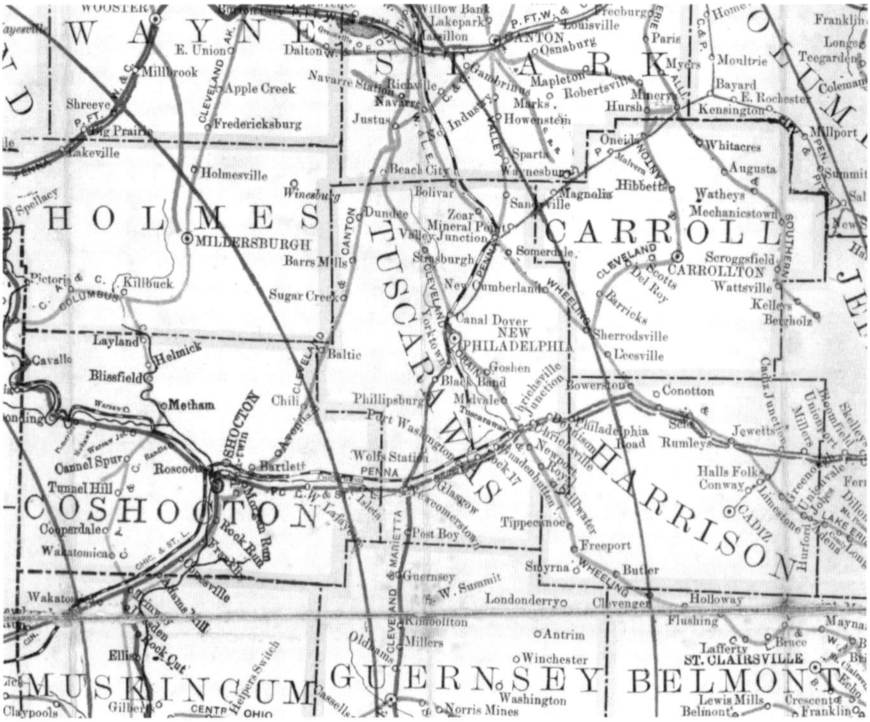

A railroad map of Tuscarawas County and surrounding counties, 1895. *Library of Congress, Geography and Map Division.*

The danger from the Black Hand in Tuscarawas County did not end with the arrest and imprisonment of Antonio Vicario in 1909. Only two years later, an Italian immigrant working for the railroad and living in Newcomerstown was brutally murdered by two men believed to be Black Hand extortionists. The murder frightened the entire Italian immigrant community then living in Newcomerstown and the surrounding communities. While the railroad and police investigated the case as best as they could, no one was ever arrested for his murder.

There is no way to know how many members of the Tuscarawas County community received extortion letters from the Black Hand. Unless the victims reported the letters to the police or perhaps a news reporter, there would be no public record. That the Black Hand continued to exist after 1911, and expand its illicit activities, is clearly obvious from newspaper accounts all across Ohio. A double shooting in Dennison in the spring of 1918 was attributed to the Black Hand. During the summer of 1924, the

Italian immigrant community in Newcomerstown was flooded with Black Hand letters, each demanding $1,000 from the recipients. Incidents of Black Hand murders, bombings, shootings, intimidation of public officials and extortion were regularly reported on, though no Black Hand murders were reported to have occurred in the local community since 1911. That changed in 1925.

Pietro Rossi (Peter Ross) emigrated from Italy to the United States in 1909 and found work as a member of a railroad work crew. That work brought him to Ohio by 1910, and his wife, Carmella (Carrie), joined him there from Italy shortly afterward. After the arrival of his wife, Peter found a job working for the National Fireproofing Brick Plant south of Magnolia, Ohio. Magnolia, and its surrounding industries, straddled the Stark-Carroll-Tuscarawas County lines. Through his hard work and efforts, Peter was eventually promoted to foreman, and he and his wife rented a home on Magnolia Road, just south of town, in a neighborhood known as Blocktown. His success encouraged his two brothers to immigrate to America as well. One of the brothers lived with Peter and his wife while the other worked and lived in Canton.

Peter, Carrie and the brother went for a drive after attending church on Sunday, August 23, 1925. When they arrived back at the Ross home, the two passengers exited and went into the house while Peter parked the car in the garage. As he neared the back of the driveway by the house, a man came out of the bushes and fired his double-barreled shotgun into the car. Peter Ross was killed instantly. There was no record of Peter Ross receiving a Black Hand letter, but his success in America certainly made him an obvious target. Newspaper accounts of the murder never mention the Black Hand or that they were suspected of the crime. However, when Peter was buried at Saint Mary's of Morges Catholic Cemetery, his headstone was inscribed with the words "Killed by Italian Black Hands." No one was ever charged with Peter Ross's murder, and ominously, the engraved quote has been defaced since his burial.

Organized crime in Ohio, including those who might be associated with the Black Hand, gravitated into other illicit activities as the United States progressed through the era of Prohibition and into the Great Depression. The Black Hand stopped being an entity of its own and slowly faded into history as the rise of more recognizable organized crime syndicates took its place. Nonetheless, the Black Hand left their mark on the Italian immigrant community in and around Tuscarawas County.

1908
A FINAL RIDE: THE KNISELY-SPACH TRAGEDY

Arline Knisely (1891–1908) was the daughter of New Philadelphia, Ohio carpenter and builder Benjamin Franklin Knisely (1852–1916) and his wife, Anna Laura (1857–1942). The Knisely family lived on the 400 block of North Broadway, and their three daughters attended school in New Philadelphia. After completing school, Arline found work in Akron as a ticket seller at the Grand Theater, a nickelodeon operated by estranged New Philadelphia couple Charles (1861–1908) and Mary Spach (1860–1935).

Charles and Mary Spach owned a home on the 300 block of North Sixth Street (modern Third Street NW) in New Philadelphia, where Mary lived with the couple's son John (1885–1911). Prior to Mary acquiring the lease on the theater in Akron around 1906, Charles made his living as a paper hanger and painter. It is possible he knew the Knisely family as a result of his previous occupation. Charles now, with assistance of another man, operated the theater in Akron and likely hired Arline as the ticket taker there. Interestingly, and perhaps the reason for the Spachs' estrangement, according to the 1908 Akron City Directory, Arline and Charles lived at the same address in Akron in 1908.

Arline Knisely returned to New Philadelphia from Akron to visit with her family at the beginning of June 1908. Charles Spach decided to return to New Philadelphia around the same time and visited with Arline and her family at their home on Friday, June 19, 1908. That evening, Charles rented a buggy from the Eckert Livery Stable and picked up Arline at her home. The two went for a ride through the nearby residential neighborhoods. As the buggy passed the Evans home on North Sixth Street, sixteen-year-old Virginia Evans (1892–1946) heard a woman cry out and then gunshots. The buggy continued past the house and then turned east on Park Avenue and, before the vehicle abruptly wheeled around and returned east, Charles Spach's body fell from it.

The buggy turned south onto North Sixth Street and was stopped by two men in front of the Utterback residence, where they discovered Arline's body drooped over the front of the buggy. When the police arrived, they discovered that both Arline and Charles had been shot in the head at close range, and a revolver with four empty chambers was found on the floor of the buggy. Arline was dead; Charles was near dead. Before losing consciousness, Charles said that the shooting was his fault but then stated that one of his theater partners had pulled the trigger. As the police believed Charles was near death, they took him to his nearby home to be nursed by his wife, Mary. The man he named as his shooter was German immigrant Robert C. Stueve.

Authorities took Robert C. Stueve into custody quickly, only to learn that he had an alibi that placed him in Cleveland the night of the shooting. In the meantime, authorities learned that Charles Spach was infatuated with Arline, a girl young enough to be his daughter. Prior to Charles picking up Arline for the buggy ride, those who came into contact with him stated that he was agitated and out of sorts. Any romantic relationship that Charles and Arline may have had before that Friday night in June 1908 may have been ended by the young and vivacious Arline during her fateful buggy ride.

Charles Spach, after making what appeared to be a brief recovery, was arrested and soon taken from his home to Union Hospital in an effort to remove the bullet still lodged in his skull. Charles Spach did not survive the attempt, and on the evening of Tuesday, June 22, 1908, he died from his wounds. The subsequent coroner's inquest attributed Arline and Charles's deaths to a murder-suicide and closed the case. Whatever transpired between Arline Knisely and Charles Spach in that rented buggy on North Sixth Street was never definitively discerned.

1909

SURVIVING THE SHADOWS: THE SHOOTING OF GIOVANNI MESI

One fateful evening in Mineral City, Ohio, marked the beginning of one Italian immigrant's journey in a new land—a journey that very nearly ended that night as well.

In 1909, Giovanni Mesi had only been in the United States for a couple of years when he found himself working on a moonlit night as the watchman at the Mineral City Tunnel of the Cleveland & Pittsburgh Railroad. When the night was over, he was in the hospital, stabbed and shot twice, and the body of one of his assailants lay in the morgue. Whether Mesi would survive his wounds was unknown at the time.

Giovanni Mesi was born in the small town of Isnello on the island of Sicily in July 1884. Very little about his life there is known other than the names of his parents and a couple of his siblings. One of those siblings, a brother named Antonio Mesi, immigrated to the United States shortly before Giovanni's immigration in 1907. The evidence for this is the passenger manifest for the SS *Moltke*. Antonio was recorded as the relative Giovanni was going to be joining in America, and Mineral City was listed as Giovanni's final destination (though they called it simply Mineral, Ohio).

Antonio and Giovanni (called John now by some) both worked as laborers for the Cleveland & Pittsburgh Railroad, work that often took them to other stops along the railroad's line. At some point during a trip to Cleveland, Giovanni met fellow Italian immigrant Santa Maria Valardi. Giovanni, like many immigrants, was saving up as much of his money as he could for his new life in America, and apparently, others were aware of that as well. The evening of Monday, August 30, 1909, Giovanni was working as the night watchman at the entrance to the Mineral City tunnel. It was a clear night, and the full moon illuminated the area around the tunnel entrance.

Giovanni was sitting in the little shack provided him by the tunnel entrance when three men approached. They briefly talked, and then one of the men asked Giovanni for a drink of water. When Giovanni bent down to fill a cup from the bucket, the man struck Giovanni hard on the back of the head. Stunned, Giovanni stood up and was stabbed three times by the assailants before he could draw his own revolver from his pocket. Gunfire erupted in the shed, and Giovanni was shot twice but managed to shoot one of the robbers. After seeing their partner collapse on the floor, the other two men ran off into the darkness.

Giovanni—shot, stabbed and bleeding—crawled the nearly two miles to Mineral City to get help from the first house he came upon. The community, learning of what happened, immediately sent men to the scene of the crime to try to catch the other two perpetrators. Giovanni was placed on a train and quickly taken to the hospital in Dover, where doctors treated his wounds. While Giovanni's wounds were serious, including a bullet lodged in his lung, they were thankfully not fatal. The unidentified assailant Giovanni shot died from his wounds. The other two men who assaulted Giovanni were never apprehended.

A month after the attack, Giovanni married Santa Valardi, and a couple of years later, the couple moved to Columbus, Ohio. There Giovanni continued to work for railroads for the rest of life. He became a naturalized citizen and raised seven children with his wife. Santa Valardi Mesi died in 1967 at the age of seventy-eight, and Giovanni Mesi survived her by six years, dying in 1973 at the age of eighty-eight. They are both buried in Saint Joseph Cemetery in Franklin County, Ohio. Giovanni Mesi's American Dream almost ended on that moonlit night in Mineral City in 1909.

1910

GUILTY UNTIL PROVEN INNOCENT: JOHN WILLIAMS AND THE BOLIVAR BANK BLAST

After someone blew up the Bolivar State Bank attempting to crack its safe on October 31, 1910, authorities zeroed in on one suspect in particular. He was a lifelong burglar just out of the penitentiary, but did they have the right man?

There is a great challenge to tracking down lifelong criminals, especially in an era when identification could be minimal at best. John Williams (1882–?), assuming that was his real name, is a great case in point. According to the 1910 U.S. Census, when Williams was incarcerated in the Ohio State Penitentiary, he claimed he was born to an Ohioan father and Michigander mother in 1882. Williams was living (and burglarizing) in the Canton/Massillon area by 1903 and was using any number of aliases, including John Wells, John Welch, John Welsh, John Conners, Harry Welch and Harry Wells.

In 1903, there were dozens of burglaries in Stark County, Ohio, that had the authorities stumped. While investigating one burglary in January 1904, officers arrested Williams, who was in possession of a firearm and a chisel that matched the tool used to break open a window in one of the burglaries. When Williams arrived in court for his hearing, he was wearing a suit he had burglarized from the home of one of the lawyers present at the proceedings. Ultimately, Stark County believed he was responsible for over forty burglaries, and in order to avoid a life sentence, Williams pleaded guilty to the one burglary and was sentenced to ten years in the Ohio State Penitentiary.

Williams was released from the Ohio State Penitentiary in September 1910, a few years earlier than his sentence. After a brief stop in New Philadelphia, where he and a partner were run out for panhandling, he returned to Stark County. His return was big news, and the newspapers reported on it, though this time using another one of his aliases, John Welch. Williams claimed to be looking for work and insisted that he was no longer living a life of crime. Canton officials were unconvinced, and on October 25, 1910, they ordered him to leave the city. Williams left willingly, believing that "he would be blamed for every theft in the city" if he stayed in Canton.

Six days later, in the early morning hours of October 31, 1910, three explosions in the course of one hour were heard in the town of Bolivar, Ohio. Despite the noise, no one in town ventured out to learn the cause, and it was not until morning that it was discovered someone had attempted to blow open the safe inside the Bolivar State Bank. The bank, at that time, was located inside the wood-frame Knights of Pythias building, and the explosions blew out the building's windows, damaged the furniture and sent an adding machine into the street, but the burglars were unable to open the bank's Deibold Safe & Lock Company safe. The timing could not have been worse for John Williams.

The Ohio State Penitentiary, Columbus, Ohio, circa 1905. *Library of Congress Prints and Photographs Division, Washington, D.C.*

Canal Street, Bolivar, Ohio, circa 1910. *Tuscarawas County Historical Society.*

A burglary occurred in nearby Magnolia the same evening as the Bolivar State Bank burglary attempt, and a man matching the description of the recently released serial burglar John Williams was reported to have been dining in a café there that night. Needless to say, Stark County officials immediately pinned the Magnolia and Bolivar State Bank burglaries on John Williams, under his alias of John Welch. Williams was arrested and brought to Canton for questioning on both crimes. Williams maintained his innocence, even under intense pre-Miranda questioning by police.

After two months of investigations, authorities were unable to uncover evidence to tie Williams to the Bolivar State Bank blast. Instead, and hoping to get the life sentence they believed Williams deserved, they sent charges against him for the Magnolia burglary to a grand jury. That grand jury refused to indict Williams, and looking for another angle, authorities then decided to charge him for the ten-year-old burglary of the lawyer's belongings. It was now April 1911, and law enforcement in Toledo arrested a statewide ring of twelve bank robbers that they believed was responsible for the failed 1910 Bolivar State Bank burglary. Those burglars went to trial in June 1911, and within days, a judge ordered the release of John Williams on his own recognizance.

My attempts to track down John Williams, alias John Welch et al., after his release in June 1911, have proven fruitless. His many aliases make it difficult. I can only hope that he truly did give up his life of crime.

1911

THE UNSOLVED MURDER OF ANTONIO D'ALASSANDRO

The story of America is a story of waves of immigration. During the late 1800s and the early 1900s, that wave consisted principally of immigrants from central and southern Europe. These immigrants, in their search for a better life in America, brought with them aspects of their previous lives in Europe. Religion, language and culture all made the voyage with them. The murder of Antonio D'Alassandro highlighted something else that came with them.

On the morning of December 1, 1911, following an evening of socializing, the Italian immigrants who worked for the railroad went to wake their friend, who was sleeping in a bunkhouse boxcar a few cars down from them. They knocked on the door and called out his name, but there was no answer from inside the boxcar. Figuring that their friend was still sleeping off the night's festivities, they went in to rouse him from his slumber. When they entered the boxcar, they were greeted with a terrible sight.

Antonio D'Alassandro (1868–1911) immigrated to the United States in 1905, leaving his wife and family behind in Italy. Like many immigrants, he came alone to establish himself so that, in the future, he would be able to bring his family to the United States as well. Antonio secured work as a laborer on the railroad systems that crisscrossed Pennsylvania and Ohio and found himself often on the move to wherever the railroads needed him. Like many other immigrants, Antonio adopted a more Americanized nickname, Tony Allison, and he would go by both names in the historic record. Antonio was living in Newcomerstown in 1910, renting a room in home on Clow Avenue with a large number of other Italian immigrants.

The scene inside of the boxcar was horrific. Antonio lay half in his bunk and half out, blood splattered the walls, the table, even the face of his pocket watch. On the floor was a bloody sledgehammer, the murder weapon, that had been used to crush Antonio's skull. His fellow workers immediately called for a doctor and law enforcement to come to the scene. After arriving, Marshal Ira Stoffer (1878–1955) investigated the scene and interviewed Antonio's acquaintances. The county coroner was notified, and he arrived in the afternoon to conduct his own investigation of the murder scene.

After interviewing Antonio's friends, Marshal Stoffer learned that Antonio had saved almost $700 in a bank account in Pittsburgh and that he regularly sent money to his family in Italy. The night of his murder, he allegedly had $100 in his possession that he was intending to deposit in the bank the next time work took him to Pittsburgh. The witnesses also reported that Antonio had gone into town earlier in the evening and returned with a stranger, another Italian immigrant, the others did not recognize. This stranger, when the time came to go to bed, went with Antonio to his boxcar. All of the witnesses were able to give a good description of this stranger to Marshal Stoffer.

The newspapers, and law enforcement, immediately believed that Antonio's murder was merely a robbery gone badly. However, the Italian community in Newcomerstown were convinced that the murder was the work of the Black Hand. Operatives of the Black Hand were extortionists within the Italian immigrant community, the organization having made its way to the United States along with its countrymen, and they were active wherever Italian immigrants resided. Typically, a letter would be sent by the Black Hand to the party being extorted, threatening harm or death to the individual if they refused to pay. Antonio's acquaintances were convinced that the stranger who murdered Antonio was a Black Hand extortionist who knew of the money Antonio possessed and saved.

The railroad's own police force had a different theory to explain Antonio's murder. They reported that, several months earlier, Antonio had denied a request from a young man in Italy to marry his daughter. The railroad's investigator believed that the young man, seeking to convince Antonio to change his mind, traveled to America. He felt that this young man was the stranger they sought. Antonio was murdered, the investigator claimed, because he again refused the young man's request for his daughter's hand.

Antonio D'Alassandro's body and belongings were turned over to a Newcomerstown undertaker to be held until the authorities determined what to do with his remains. Antonio was eventually buried, along with his earthly possessions, two weeks later in a pauper's grave despite the fact that he had $700 in the bank. No information about what happened to Antonio's savings was ever given, and Antonio's killer was never brought to justice.

1912

RUFFLED FEATHERS: A GUNFIGHT AT THE COUNTY JAIL

Early in the evening on a cold February night in 1912, neighbors of the Tuscarawas County Jail on East Fair Street in New Philadelphia heard the sounds of gunfire ring out. It was the exclamation point on a busy and successful weekend by local law enforcement, having broken up a large gambling event two days earlier. This is the story of the men involved and how that gunfight happened.

During the first decade of the 1900s, there was a coal mine operating along the Goshen–Fairfield Township line in Tuscarawas County called the Mullins mine. Around that mine, a small community of miners and those who served them called "Egypt" or "Little Egypt" grew. One of the people who established a business in the small community was a man named Hamilton Beans (1874–1919). Beans operated a store and saloon in the community, catering to the men who worked in the Mullins Mine. Beans also operated a saloon on North Broadway in New Philadelphia, Ohio, as well.

The evening of Saturday, February 24, 1912, men from all over the county gathered at Beans's saloon in Little Egypt to watch, and wager, on a number of cockfights. Over sixty people from across the county attended the fights, and there were at least twenty-three fighting roosters slated to take part. County law enforcement was informed that the fights were taking place and raided Beans's establishment late Saturday into early Sunday morning. They took the names of all of those in attendance, charged Beans with a handful of crimes and confiscated all of the fighting birds.

Mullins Mine, Little Egypt, Ohio, circa the early twentieth century. *Tuscarawas County Historical Society.*

New Philadelphia, Ohio officials and policemen, circa the early twentieth century. *Tuscarawas County Historical Society.*

The Monday after the fight, the roosters were taken to the Tuscarawas County Jail and locked in a stall in the jail's stable at the rear of the lot. Local law enforcement was concerned that the various owners of the valuable fighting birds might try to recover their property under cover of darkness. They decided to post an armed guard in the stable to make sure that did not happen. The man who drew the first shift was a Minnesota-born transplant to Ohio named Patrick Henry (1891–1965), a twenty-one-year-old deputy patrolman who had been in New Philadelphia only a short time. Around six o'clock that evening, Henry climbed into a buggy in the barn, wrapped himself in a blanket and kept his eyes and ears open.

Despite Henry's short time in New Philadelphia, the local newspaper reported favorably that he had "made an enviable record for himself," that he had "the traits of a true officer" and was "fearless." Two hours into Henry's shift, he heard the sounds of someone forcing the large stable doors open and moved into a position where he could better see the stall holding the confiscated birds. From the dark, he saw a man strike a match and look around the stable. The man tried unsuccessfully to force open the stall door; that was when Henry turned on his flashlight and shone it on the perpetrator. Officer Henry ordered the man to put his hands up and accompany him to the mayor's office.

What happened next became fodder for later debate. The man attempting to break into the stall and recover the fighting birds was a New Philadelphia coal miner named Howard Torgler (1879–1968). Torgler, a respected member of the community, lived just a block away from the jail on East Ray Street with his wife and children. The press wrote at the time that they believed he had been asked by some of the birds' owners to try to recover their property. Another report wrote that he may have been trying to recover a bird of his own. Which story was accurate is still a mystery.

Needless to say, Torgler did not comply with Officer Henry's order. According to Henry, Torgler ran out of the stable and slammed the door in Henry's face as he gave chase. Officer Henry stated that, once outside in the jail yard, Torgler drew a .32-caliber pistol and fired in his direction. The shot missed Henry, and the officer drew his own firearm and fired twice at Torgler, grazing him in the left leg. Torgler, though wounded, fired two more rounds at Officer Henry's head but missed. Henry, as Torgler tried to run off, fired twice more. This time he hit Torgler in the right arm, causing him to drop his gun. By this time the two men were in the middle of North Third Street (modern Second Street NW), and Henry had managed to catch up to Torgler. Torgler lunged at Henry, but the officer was able strike Torgler

The Tuscarawas County Jail, New Philadelphia, Ohio, circa 1920. *Tuscarawas County Historical Society.*

on the head with his nightstick. Two other officers arrived on the scene and were finally able to subdue Torgler.

Despite Torgler's injury, he was taken into the county jail overnight. Rumors began to swell almost immediately that a mob was going to form at the jail and planned to lynch the newcomer Henry for shooting a longtime resident of the city. The mayor and sheriff attempted to lower the temperature by expressing support for Officer Henry's actions in the gunfight, but they were concerned about the possibility of mob violence against Henry and posted men with riot guns and 220 rounds of ammunition at the jail. Henry, for his part, was unfazed by the threats and returned to his post in the stable after turning over Torgler's firearm to the police chief.

Howard Torgler was taken before the mayor the next day and charged with attempted burglary and shooting with intent to kill. Friends, including Hamilton Beans, helped him post bail, and he was released later that day. Torgler claimed that Officer Henry had not identified himself as a peace officer, had fired first and that he had simply fired in an effort to defend himself against an unknown assailant. A later newspaper article about the event painted a sympathetic picture of Howard Torgler's situation, a local well-known resident injured and unable to work and suffering from blood poisoning as a result of his arm injury.

The historical record that survives seems to indicate that it was ultimately Howard Torgler, the longtime resident, whose story was believed over that of the recent arrival. There is no record of Torgler being charged by a grand jury or tried for any crime related to the gunfight. Officer Patrick Henry, it would seem, was dismissed from his position as a peace officer, because later that year, he sued the City of New Philadelphia for wages due to him while he served. The newspapers are interestingly silent about the event after the fact, indicating that the situation was handled quietly.

Hamilton Beans, the alleged host of the cockfight that started the whole mess, lived for only another seven years. He died from pneumonia in March 1919. Henry Torgler eventually regained his health and returned to coal mining before being hired by the state highway department. He died in New Philadelphia in February 1968. Patrick Henry, who had "the traits of a true officer," moved to Stark County, where he ended up a party to a series of car thefts. He was convicted and served time in the Ohio State Reformatory in Mansfield. After his release, he returned to his home state of Minnesota but died in Yuma, Arizona, in 1965.

1912

"MORTO ASSASINATO": THE MURDER OF FRANCESCO FANTIN

Francesco Fantin (1872–1912) first came to America in the summer of 1891 and spent six years in the United States before returning to Italy around 1897. It is possible that, during those six years, he was working in Ohio, though it is difficult to confirm. Upon returning to his hometown of Barcis, Italy, he married Sabadina Pinor (1874–1951) in 1899, and a little over a year later, the couple welcomed a son. Francesco decided to return to America, this time with his young family, and the three arrived in New York in November 1906.

According to the Fantins' paperwork, they intended to make Dennison, Ohio, their destination, as Francesco's cousin was already living there. It is possible that Francesco and his cousin traveled together when Francesco came to America the first time in 1891. Francesco decided instead to settle near Roswell, Ohio, and found work in the coal mines nearby. The Fantin family expanded by 1912 to include three more sons and a daughter. Francesco became a respected member of the Roswell community and a member of the New Philadelphia Loyal Order of the Moose. Four years after returning to the United States, in May 1910, Francesco Fantin became a U.S. citizen.

One of the Fantins' Union Township neighbors was coal miner and constable Sherman Bartholomew (1862–1920). Bartholomew came from an established Tuscarawas County family and, despite being a constable, was a hothead and troublemaker who had been arrested before for destruction of property and assaulting three boys while serving in his role as constable. Bartholomew was quick to show a gun and threaten violence when he felt provoked. Francesco Fantin would find out just how quick late on the evening of September 22, 1912.

Bartholomew and Fantin were walking past the post office in Roswell around 11:30 p.m. when Joshua Lemasters (1866–1925) and Peter Paulus (1865–1946) pulled up in Lemasters's buggy. The four men began talking, and when the conversation turned to politics, things became heated between Bartholomew and Paulus. Paulus struck Bartholomew and sent him sprawling to the ground. According to Paulus and Lemasters, Fantin tried to defuse the situation and went over to offer Bartholomew a hand up. That was when Bartholomew drew a revolver and fired, striking Fantin in the stomach. Francesco Fantin died on the road in front of the Roswell post office.

Bartholomew showed little remorse for killing Fantin, stating, "I'm not ashamed of what I done," and "He came at me and I shot." Bartholomew claimed self-defense in the killing of Fantin, despite witness testimony to the contrary. It also likely helped Bartholomew's case with the public that the press repeatedly referred to Fantin as a "foreigner" and an "Italian" despite him being a naturalized U.S. citizen. After a brief trial, Bartholomew was found guilty of manslaughter and sentenced to up to ten years in prison. Bartholomew appealed and did not see the inside of the Ohio State Penitentiary until July 1913. Upon being sentenced, Bartholomew claimed he would be out of jail in a year's time.

View of Roswell, Ohio, 1923. *Tuscarawas County Historical Society.*

Bartholomew's estimate of how long he would serve was close, as he was released in December 1914, after serving less than a year and a half. He died from cancer six years later. Francesco Fantin was buried at East Avenue Cemetery in New Philadelphia, Ohio, where his headstone read "Morto Assasinato" or "Murdered Dead." Sabadina Fantin never remarried and raised the couple's five children in the Roswell area. Sabadina died in May 1951. Francesco and Sabadina sought a better life in America for themselves, their five children and their eventual eighteen grandchildren. Despite Francesco's violent death in 1912 at the hands of a remorseless constable, the Fantin family thrived in America.

1913

ONE DRINK TOO MANY: THE CANTON HOUSE KILLING

John Brant Sr. (1852–1926) was born in Germany and arrived in New York City in 1868 or 1869. Shortly after his arrival, he married Mary Ortman (1852–1920), and a few years later their eldest son, John Brant Jr. (1874–1923), was born in Manhattan, New York. John Sr. was a furniture maker and soon moved his family from New York to Columbus, Ohio, where he eventually opened his own furniture store. John Jr. worked there in a variety of roles, eventually as a buyer on behalf of his father.

It is possible that John Jr. met West Virginia–born Mary Simmons (1876–aft. 1936) when she worked as a housekeeper in a rooming house in Columbus, Ohio, though she relocated to Uhrichsville before the couple were married in Tuscarawas County in March 1913. John Jr., perhaps with financial assistance from his father, purchased a home on East Fourth Street in Uhrichsville that had previously been known as the "Canton House." He set out immediately in making repairs in preparation for returning it to its role as a hotel and boardinghouse.

On the night of Saturday, December 6, 1913, Ralph Jordan (1888–1913); his twin brother, Roy Jordan (1888–1963); Robert Hutson (1883–1980); and Roy Johnson (1880–1927) were all drinking at Dennison's Douglas Saloon after a hard day's work at the Royal Brick Works in Midvale. Eventually, the men became so intoxicated that the saloon's owner, George Douglas (1872–1955), was forced to kick them out. After leaving the saloon, Roy Jordan parted ways with his brother Ralph and the other two men as they headed to Uhrichsville, where Hutson and Johnson both lived.

Meanwhile, John Brant was busy working on the plumbing in his home on East Fourth Street in Uhrichsville when he heard loud noises coming from the rear of the house at around 10:00 pm. Given the lateness of the hour, John thought it best to put his .38-caliber revolver in his pocket before going to investigate. When John stepped out onto the back porch, he saw three men in the yard and told them they needed to leave. The three men were the intoxicated and belligerent Ralph Jordan and his friends Robert Hutson and Roy Johnson.

After John Brant confronted the three men in his backyard, Ralph Jordan stepped up onto the porch and struck John in the face, knocking him into the yard. Jordan then struck Brant a second time, knocking him to his knees against the wall of a building behind the home. Jordan then allegedly said, "I'll kick your damn face in!" And it was at that point that the kneeling, bleeding and stunned John Brant drew his revolver and fired two shots at Jordan. Jordan fell to the ground, and Hutson and Johnson ran off. Jordan died from his wounds a couple of hours later.

John Brant turned himself in shortly after the shooting and was housed in the Tuscarawas County Jail, charged with first-degree murder for several days, before being released on bail provided by his father. A month after the killing, a grand jury refused to indict John Brant, arguing that his shooting of Ralph Jordan that night was in self-defense and not murder. Three months later, John Brant sold the Uhrichsville property, and he and Mary moved to Florida. John Brant died in Florida in January 1923, and Mary Simmons Brant remarried two years later.

1919

"SURE, I SHOT HIM": MURDER ON PANHANDLE #34

The state of Ohio was, and still is, crisscrossed with railroad tracks and routes. While the heyday of railroad passenger travel has long since left Ohio, in the early twentieth century, it was abundant. Those passengers often found themselves traveling through Tuscarawas County on their way to destinations east and west. Sometimes those trains were the scenes of crimes—crimes that would be tried in Tuscarawas County. This is one of those cases.

Nicholas Chambers (1843–1919) was born on the Fourth of July 1843, likely in Hancock County, Ohio, where his parents owned a large farm. He was one of at least ten children of William (1811–1889) and Keziah (1821–1903) Chambers, who both reported their birth as having been in Ohio as well. The family had relocated to Wyandot County, Ohio, just as the Civil War was beginning, and it was here where Nicholas enlisted in the Company F, 123rd Ohio Volunteer Infantry Regiment. Nicholas would serve throughout the war in the Virginia theater and survived to return home to his family.

Nicholas married Werlinda Ollam (1843–1915) in Delaware County, Ohio, in 1867 and began to raise his own family there. The couple welcomed their first and only child, a son, James, in 1872. The family lived, by all appearances, a quiet farm life and operated a hardware store in Concord, Delaware County. James eventually moved to Maryland, where he opened and ran a successful store, and Werlinda passed away in 1915, leaving Nicholas a widower. Nicholas was on his way to visit his son in Maryland in May 1919 when he encountered fellow rail passenger Frank Seinich.

Artist's rendering based on a period photograph of murderer Frank Seinich, 2024. *Courtesy of Luc Poirier.*

Very little is known about the early years of Frank Seinich (1889–1919) other than he was born in Austria-Hungary. His sister and her husband immigrated to the United States in 1903 and settled in Chicago, Illinois. Six years later, Frank followed his sister to America and, in 1910, was living with her and her husband in Chicago, where he worked as a trimmer in a tailor shop. According to later newspaper accounts, Frank was a "confessed Bolshevik" with communist sympathies, though that is difficult to confirm. Seinich decided that he was done with Chicago and was on his way to find new work in Philadelphia in May 1919.

Frank Seinich was already on board the eastbound Pittsburgh, Cincinnati, Chicago and St. Louis Railroad #34 passenger train when seventy-two-year-old Nicholas Chambers boarded at Plain City. Unbeknownst to him at the time, Chambers made the mistake of sitting with the towering two-hundred-pound Austrian. At some point on the route, the train passed another loaded with American troops returning from Europe. Chambers, being the patriotic veteran that he was, loudly cheered the men as the train passed. Seinich took offense and began a heated argument with Chambers about the war and America's role in it. This loud argument continued as their train passed Newcomerstown.

Nicholas Chambers, the Civil War veteran born on the Fourth of July, finally tired of what he perceived to be Seinich's unpatriotic argument and dismissively waved his hand at Seinich. According to some witnesses, Chambers told Seinich, "Let's quit arguing. Go away. I don't want to talk with you." Another witness reported that Chambers told Seinich to "shut up." Regardless of what was said, Seinich was enraged. He left his seat, walked a short distance down the aisle, drew a revolver, turned and fired three shots into the head and neck of Nicholas Chambers at point-blank range.

Passengers in the car scrambled to get out and away from the gunman. Once the car was empty of everyone but Seinich and his victim, it was locked, trapping Seinich in the car. After the train pulled into Dennison, a railroad detective boarded and took Seinich into custody without incident. Seinich, during his arraignment, claimed that he feared that the elderly

Postcard image of the Ohio State Penitentiary electric chair, circa the early twentieth century. *Image courtesy of author.*

Chambers might have shot or stabbed him, so, "Sure I shot him," he told the court. Seinich was taken to the jail in New Philadelphia to await his next court appearance.

Frank Seinich had admitted to the murder of Nicholas Chambers, and all that was left to do was gather witness testimony and pronounce sentencing. Witnesses were interviewed during the months of May and June, some now claiming that they had subdued Seinich on the train. Seinich's associations with communists and labor unions (synonymous at the time) were highlighted in the press, as was his mental state. The newspapers reported that Seinich prayed a great deal and regularly requested the presence of a local priest in his cell. The evidence and testimony concluded, Seinich was sentenced in early July 1919 to death by electrocution. Ohio, in 1897, was the second state to adopt the use of the electric chair for performing executions, and it was only the second time since 1825 that a death sentence had been handed down in a Tuscarawas County courtroom.

The judge set Seinich's date of execution for Friday, October 17, 1919, and ordered Seinich sent to the state penitentiary to await his fate. According to newspaper accounts in the days leading up to his execution, Seinich feigned insanity and had to be force-fed his meals. The day of his execution, Frank Seinich calmly entered the "death chamber" attended by a number of priests. The chiefs of police of Uhrichsville and New Philadelphia attended the execution. Seinich was not permitted any proverbial last words. Frank Seinich took his seat in the chair and, within a few seconds, was electrocuted to death.

Two strangers boarded the Pittsburgh, Cincinnati, Chicago and St. Louis Railroad #34 passenger train on May 7, 1919—a train ride that ended for both of them in Tuscarawas County and cost both men their lives. Nicholas Chambers is buried in Plain City, Ohio, and his murderer, Frank Seinich, is buried twenty miles away in Mount Calvary Cemetery in Columbus, Ohio.

1919

MYSTERY IN DOVER: THE MURDER OF DOMENICO VERSACE

The story of the murder of a young Italian immigrant, new to the country and recently married, is a mystery on many levels—a mystery yet to be solved that raises more questions than answers.

Four teenage neighborhood boys walked southeast along the railroad tracks between South and Railroad Avenues in Dover, Ohio, in the early hours of November 5, 1919. As they approached a spur that led to the Dover Wood Face Company buildings, they noticed the form of a man lying along the railroad tracks. It was one o'clock in the morning, and the boys at first thought the man might have been intoxicated and simply fallen asleep. As they got closer, they observed a pool of blood around the man that indicated something more sinister.

The boys ran to get help at the home of Dover policeman Daniel Peacock (1856–1932), who lived on nearby Shafer Avenue. Peacock quickly determined that the man was dead and had been shot several times, leaving a large pool of blood around his body. Peacock had the body taken to the morgue of the Dover furniture maker and undertaker Christian Keuerleber (1864–1947) on West Third Street in Dover, where it was examined by a doctor and justice of the peace, John S. Gordon (1848–1931). Their examination concluded that the victim had been shot six times: the first two shots severed the femoral artery in his leg and the last four were fired into his torso as he lay dying.

The authorities identified the victim as an Italian immigrant and the son-in-law of Frank Longo (or Long), another Italian immigrant living in Dover. The name of the victim reported in the newspaper was given in a few different and confusing ways: Domineck Elpastro, Domineck Celcastro, Dominick Celcastro and, on his death certificate, Domenick (Versaci) Celestro. According to Frank Longo, the deceased was married to Longo's daughter Angelina about a year earlier in Cleveland, Ohio, and had only recently arrived in Dover and found work at the Penn Iron and Coal Company.

The twenty-four-year-old victim immigrated to the United States in 1910 from his hometown of Reggio Calabria, a town on the very tip of the Italian "boot" directly across the Strait of Messina from Sicily. Arriving first in New York, he made his way to Cleveland, where the Longo family were also living before they relocated to Dover. It was while in Cleveland that he met Angelina, and the two were married sometime before he declared his intention to become a U.S. citizen in April 1919. The name on that declaration was recorded as Domenico Versace, and after signing his declaration, the couple moved to Dover, Ohio.

Domenico was buried in St. Joseph's Cemetery on Friday, November 7, 1919, even as the investigation into his death continued. No money had been taken from the body, and his pockets had not been turned out in search of anything worth stealing. It was determined that Angelina was in no way involved and had no knowledge of who killed her husband. The authorities stated they believed they knew who the killer was and that he had returned to a larger city after the murder. There had also been a handful of other killings in the local Italian immigrant community in the weeks before and after Domenico's murder. Ultimately, they determined that Domenico's death had been the settling of some kind of grudge between immigrants.

Despite authorities claiming to know the identity of the killer, no one was ever arrested and charged for the murder of Domenico Versace. After his death, Angelina returned to live in her father's home in Dover. The Longos later moved to Summit County and then Columbus, Ohio, where they lived out the remainder of their years. The questions of why Domenico was killed, why the newspaper and authorities provided different names for the victim during the period of investigation and, of course, who killed Domenico were never answered. Any American Dream that Domenico possessed was killed along with him that cold November night on those railroad tracks in Dover.

1920

VICTIM'S HEAD COULD NOT BE FOUND

We are used to seeing and hearing sensationalized headlines designed to make us click a link, pick up a magazine or "come back after the commercial break." The stories rarely live up to the hype of the headline, present outright falsehoods or tell a completely different story than the headline would have you assume. Perhaps the headline to this post did just that, and that was the entire point. What happened to Thomas K. Addy in 1920 likely sold a lot of newspapers when the headline announcing his death was printed, but his death was a tragic accident.

Residents of New Philadelphia picked up their local newspaper on Wednesday, October 20, 1920, to startling headlines. "Death Veiled in Mystery," "Find Headless Body Along Track," "Money Untouched" and "Victim's Head Could Not Be Located" were emblazoned in the far-right column of the paper, above the fold. The victim's name was Thomas K. Addy (1864–1920), and his headless, but apparently otherwise unharmed, body had been discovered by two railroad employees.

Thomas was the son of Guernsey County farmer Hugh Addy (1821–1903) and his wife, Margaret Warden (1832–1898). Thomas came from a very large family and, along with his siblings, was working on his father's farm by the age of fifteen. After his own marriage to Ida Hutchison (1869–1963) in 1891, he was farming and raising his own family in Guernsey County. Farming must not have suited Thomas because, in 1910, his household lived in Oxford Township, Tuscarawas County, and Thomas worked in a local brickwork.

In 1920, Thomas and his family lived about two miles south of Newcomerstown, close to a tunnel on the Cleveland & Marietta Railroad line. Thomas had returned to farming but also worked as the tunnel's night watchman. This job required him to make sure that the tracks in the tunnel were free of any debris, as well as to prevent potential collisions between trains. It was likely that his duties as the watchman placed him near the tracks the evening before his body was found.

It was around one o'clock on Wednesday morning, and two Cleveland & Marietta Railroad employees were walking along the tracks near the tunnel south of Newcomerstown. The two men noticed a body a short distance away from the tunnel entrance and tracks. As the men approached the body, they saw that the head was completely gone. The men searched the dead man's pockets and discovered that nothing had been stolen; his pocket watch and wallet, containing $150, were intact. They also claimed that the body had no other apparent, visible injuries.

The newspaper did a very nice job in shrouding what happened to Thomas Addy in as much mystery as possible. Careful readers, though, would have noticed that the answer was likely very simple. If it was foul play, why weren't Thomas's watch and cash stolen? How could the men who found Thomas tell if a fully-clothed man had no other injuries? It did not take long for the authorities to solve the "mystery" of Thomas Addy's death.

Only a few hours after the newspaper was printed, men working on a Cleveland & Marietta locomotive found something shocking: Thomas Addy's head. The mystery was solved, and how Thomas died became clearer. Thomas Addy, according to his family, suffered from a chronic heart condition. The investigation into his death concluded that, while Thomas was working as tunnel warden that night, he suffered some kind of heart episode. That episode caused Thomas to stumble into, and then be struck by, the oncoming locomotive. His head was severed, and his body was thrown some distance from the tracks. A tragic accident.

When Thomas's body was found, the newspaper placed that announcement at the top of the page 1, with a flurry of sensational headlines. After the cause and circumstances of Thomas's death were determined, it warranted two short paragraphs at the bottom of page 1. One New Philadelphia newspaper placed it at the bottom of page 6. Thomas was more than just a sensational headline; he was a husband and father to eight children. Thomas Addy is buried in Saint Jacobs Lutheran Cemetery in Newcomerstown.

1921
A KILLING ON DEPOT STREET

What was supposed to be a celebratory extended family dinner in a small home of recent Italian immigrants in Dover, Ohio, was ruined by gunshots in the night. One of the family members, soon to be wed, lay dead in the middle of the street.

Panfilo Cercone (1848–aft. 1902), a widower from the town of Pettorano, along the Gizio River in Italy, came to the United States in November 1902 to join a son named Antonio then living in Dover, Ohio. Other family members followed, and among them was Panfilo's son Pasquale Cercone (1888–1921), who arrived in the United States in May 1903 and then made his way west to be with his father and siblings. Panfilo left Dover soon after Pasquale's arrival and eventually settled outside of Pittsburgh, Pennsylvania, with another of his sons.

The records of first-generation immigrants are always difficult to track in the years immediately after their arrival, but from the records that do survive, it appears that Pasquale had at least six siblings who immigrated to America in the first decade of the 1900s. At first, Pasquale settled briefly in the Youngstown area, where in 1910 he was recorded working in a steel rolling mill. At least three brothers and a sister were living in Dover that same year while another brother and Panfilo were living near Pittsburgh. Pasquale arrived in Dover around 1911 and found work with the Penn Mold Manufacturing Company, where he was working when he registered for the World War I draft in 1917.

Pasquale and one of his older brothers managed to save enough money by September 1919 to purchase a small house on the corner of West Seventh

Third and Factory Streets looking west in Dover, Ohio, circa 1910. *Tuscarawas County Historical Society.*

Street and Center Street in Dover. One of Pasquale's sisters lived nearby on Depot Street, and another brother lived around the corner on Center Street. The family gathered the evening of January 17, 1921, at Pasquale's house for a dinner to celebrate that Pasquale's fiancée was en route from Italy to join him in Dover. Pasquale excused himself from the table at one point and went outside, and within a few minutes, one of his brothers claimed to have heard two gunshots ring out.

Pasquale's brother later told authorities that he ran down West Seventh Street about two hundred yards to Depot Street and there saw his brother lying in the middle of the road. Pasquale had been shot twice in the chest, and though weak and losing blood quickly, the wounded man said he had not recognized or seen his assailant. A local ambulance was sent for to take Pasquale to Union Hospital, but he died before the ambulance arrived. The authorities began an investigation immediately, but they were already telling the press that this was likely a case of a "feud which has existed among some of Cercone's countrymen."

After several hours questioning neighbors and witnesses, including men working on the nearby railroad, the authorities identified the gunman as

Antonio Trestano (1892–1959). Trestano (sometimes spelled Tristano), also from the town of Pettorano, immigrated to the United States in 1909 and served in the Thirty-Ninth Infantry Division during World War I, where he was wounded twice in battle. Antonio claimed self-defense, stating that Pasquale had fired eleven shots at him before Antonio returned fire—an interesting claim considering that none of the other witnesses reported that they heard those eleven shots. Eleven shots would also seem to indicate that Pasquale had more than one gun or was with someone else who must have also fired at Antonio.

Despite the authorities' assumption that it was merely a "feud" among the Italian residents of Dover, there were other potential motives for the killing of Pasquale Cercone that came to light in the weeks after the murder. One hinted at letters by either Pasquale or Antonio to an unnamed woman in Italy (perhaps Pasquale's fiancée?), and another claimed that Pasquale had withdrawn a large sum of money just before the shooting. No money was reportedly found on his body (robbery?). Regardless of what the motive may have been, Antonio Trestano never denied shooting Pasquale and was charged with second-degree murder and held in the Tuscarawas County Jail until his trial date.

The brief trial of Antonio Trestano took place in May 1921, with Trestano testifying that he and Pasquale Cercone had quarreled over a suit of clothes and that Pasquale had lured Antonio to a nearby home. There, according to Antonio, Cercone fired on him eleven times and Antonio fired at Cercone in self-defense. Pasquale, of course, was not there to give his side of the story. Perhaps because of Trestano's military service and/or doubts about the honesty of the prosecution's witness testimony, the jury returned a verdict of guilty of manslaughter instead of murder. The sentence for manslaughter was one to twenty years in the Ohio Penitentiary.

Pasquale was laid to rest in St. Joseph's Cemetery in Dover, just yards from where he was killed. Two weeks after Pasquale's killing, his unnamed fiancée arrived in Dover only to learn that her future husband was dead. What happened to her is unclear. Within a few years, two more of the Cercone brothers would be dead, succumbing to tuberculosis. Antonio Trestano served less than two years in prison and eventually made his way to New York, where he married and raised a family. He died in 1959 and is buried in St. John the Baptist Cemetery in Schenectady, New York.

1921

THE BOMBING OF THE BOWERS HOUSE

Well-known attorney Henry Bowers (1858–1934) and his family had, for many years, resided on West Ray Street in New Philadelphia. Henry and his wife, Sarah "Elizabeth" Bair (1856–1936), had raised their six children in that house. However, around 1914, Henry and Sarah built a large, solid home on Tuscarawas Avenue and there they moved, along with their youngest son Russell Bowers (1891–1983) and his family.

Russell, also an attorney, was in 1921 serving as Tuscarawas County's prosecuting attorney. Russell led the county's efforts in enforcing the recently passed Eighteenth Amendment prohibiting alcohol. Not surprisingly, Tuscarawas County was not immune from bootlegging, speakeasies and illicit alcohol sales and consumption. This kept the prosecuting attorney and law enforcement very busy. While all this was going on, Russell lived in his father's house on Tuscarawas Avenue with his wife, Clelia Getz (1892–1971), and young son.

In April 1921, Prosecuting Attorney Bowers ordered a large-scale countywide raid of establishments and homes believed to be violating Prohibition law. Law enforcement swept through the cities of Dover, New Philadelphia, Dennison and Uhrichsville and arrested over forty-five individuals. Twenty-two of them were charged with crimes relating to either alcohol or operating houses of "ill repute." Among them was a Dover man named Ralph Herzig (1892–1975), son of a Swiss immigrant, who operated a saloon turned soda shop in the 300 block of Third Street.

One of Ralph's neighbors on the same block was an Italian immigrant restaurant owner whose son, Vincent "Chauncey" Nigro (1896–1922), was close to the same age as Herzig. Chauncey had served briefly during the latter months of World War I, though he never left the United States. Chauncey was, at the time of the April 1921 raids, operating his parents' restaurant and living with them on the 300 block of Third Street in Dover. Both men had been in trouble with the law, even before the April 1921 raid, for violating Prohibition by furnishing alcohol at their establishments.

Later witness testimony reported that, after the April raids, Herzig had made a number of threats against Prosecutor Bowers. One witness reported that they had seen Herzig and Nigro together and that, at that time, Herzig indicated to the witness that Nigro was going to be the one to "get that [expletive]." Early in the morning of Friday, June 10, 1921, an explosive device placed on the Bowerses' front porch detonated. The bomb tore a large hole in the wall next to the front door, ripped the front porch ceiling apart, blew out the windows in the front of the house and sent pieces of concrete and glass into the home, damaging furniture and doors inside. Luckily for the Bowerses, no one was injured in the explosion, as the family had recently vacated the downstairs bedroom.

Prosecutor Bowers and local law enforcement were aware of the threats made by Herzig and Nigro and immediately suspected them and Chauncey's father, Nick Nigro. It did not help Chauncey Nigro's case that, in the immediate aftermath of the explosion, he drove past the Bowers home multiple times and, each time, slowed and glared at the Bowers family on the front porch. Within a few days, the police believed they had gathered enough evidence to charge the men, and they were all taken into custody. All three men were, however, able to post bond and were released as they awaited trial. Prosecutor Bowers, fearing reprisal, had law enforcement officers stationed at his home armed with riot shotguns and pistols.

During the trials of the two men, Prosecutor Bowers was assisted by his father, Henry Bowers. Interestingly, Henry Bowers was best known as a defense attorney who was able to save numerous defendants from the death penalty over the course of his career. The trials of Chauncey Nigro and Ralph Herzig lasted through the summer of 1921, with both men being convicted in the bombing case. They continued to be out on bond though as their two cases made their way through the appeals processes. The prosecutor's office had yet to bring Nick Nigro's case to trial, perhaps indicating a lack of evidence of his role in the bombing.

Before Chauncey Nigro learned of the fate of his final appeal in September 1922, he allegedly killed himself in a room in Riverside Inn in Dover, Ohio. According to his girlfriend at the time, he claimed he would never go to jail and then drank an undetermined poison. Chauncey's family suspected some form of foul play, and Chauncey's death certificate did list poisoning as the cause of death without mentioning suicide. Ralph Herzig was convicted and spent three years in jail before being paroled in the summer of 1924. He returned to Dover but, in 1931, was deemed insane and sent to the Massillon State Hospital, where he stayed until after 1940. Ralph Herzig died in Massillon in 1975. After the death of Nick's son Chauncey and the conviction of Ralph Herzig, the charges against Nick Nigro were dropped, and the case of the bombing of the Bowers home drifted out of the newspapers entirely. Nick Nigro and his family continued to live in Dover, where they operated their tavern until going into the sand and coal business. Nick Nigro passed away in October 1965.

Henry Bowers continued to work as a practicing attorney, defending a number of clients, including murderers, until his death in the spring of 1934. Prosecuting Attorney Russell Bowers eventually moved his family into a large home on West Fair Avenue and continued to practice law privately with the firm of Bowers, Bowers and Mastin until his death in April 1983. The bombing of the Bowers home on Tuscarawas Avenue was one of the most violent chapters in the county's history during Prohibition and illustrated that the area was not immune to the dangers of that time.

1922

A BULLET'S PATH: THE KILLING OF BARBARA HRABLEY

Andro Hrabley (1894–1978) was born in Czechoslovakia and immigrated to the United States in 1910, first settling in Steubenville, Ohio. There he met the daughter of another immigrant family from Hungary named Barbara Svidran (1896–1922), and the couple married in 1915. The couple had two children before Andro moved the family to Dennison, Ohio, where he found work as a railroad car repairman for the railroad. They purchased a home on the 400 block of Logan Street, just across the street from the railroad yard.

Meanwhile, Giovanni (John) Russo (1884–1947) immigrated to the United States around the same time as Andro Hrabley and moved to Dennison, where he married Asunta Santa Lucia (1889–1947) sometime before 1913. The couple purchased a property on the 500 block of Logan Street, where they lived and operated a grocery store. Given the proximity of the families, their shared faith and the Russo business, it is likely they were familiar with each other.

The Hrabley family, by the time of the 1920 census, had an additional daughter in their household, born in 1918. The Russo family down the street included a son and two daughters. The children were all around the same age, and one can picture the older children attending school and playing in the neighborhood together. The 1921 Sanborn Fire Insurance Map for Dennison, Ohio, clearly showed the Russo residence's double use as a home and a neighborhood grocery.

Whether the Hrabley and Russo families knew each other well or not, they would soon be linked by a tragic and completely avoidable event.

A Tuscarawas County Courthouse courtroom interior, 1917. *Tuscarawas County Historical Society.*

The night of New Year's Eve 1921, the Hrableys were in an upstairs room in their home at around 11:30 p.m. when they heard loud noises coming from the street below from New Year's Eve revelers. According to Barbara Hrabley's later testimony, she looked out of the upstairs window, and among the people celebrating, she claimed to have seen John Russo. Barbara stated that, as she looked at him, he raised a gun and fired at her, the bullet striking her in the head.

The bullet lodged into the top of Barbara's skull, and she was quickly taken to Twin City Hospital; meanwhile, local police officers arrested John Russo. Russo claimed that he was at home at the time of the shooting and was not the person who pulled the trigger. Barbara lay in the Twin City Hospital, paralyzed on her left side with the bullet still in her head. Law enforcement, despite finding a loaded .32-caliber revolver at the Russo home, realized that there was not enough evidence to pursue a criminal case against John Russo.

Barbara Hrabley, while still in the hospital, filed a $10,000 ($188,000 today) civil case against Russo for the shooting. Eventually, surgeons were able to extract a flattened .32-caliber bullet from Barbara's head, but her paralysis was permanent. In April 1922, a jury found John Russo liable for Barbara Hrabley's injuries and awarded her the $10,000 settlement. Whether any of the money was ever paid is difficult to determine, but regardless, Barbara Hrabley died from her injury on December 4, 1922. Her cause of death was recorded as "result of gun shot wound in head." John Russo was never charged in Barbara Hrabley's death.

1924
WHAT REALLY HAPPENED? THE SHOOTING OF MRS. VESTA SNYDER

Vesta Virginia Leggett (1900–1947) was the daughter of New Philadelphia, Ohio real estate salesman Joshua F. Leggett (1854–1927) and his wife, Luella Skeeles (1861–1938). Vesta was one of nine children born to the couple between 1881 and 1906, and in 1910, the family lived just north of the Central Public School building on North Fifth Street. The family lived there at the time of Vesta's first marriage before they eventually moved into a home on West High Street in New Philadelphia.

Vesta was only sixteen years old and pregnant when she eloped to West Virginia with twenty-three-year-old New Philadelphia steel worker Russell Dean Marshall. The couple's first child, a son, was born six months later, and the young family lived in a rented house on North Sixth Street in New Philadelphia. They were living there when they welcomed their second child, another son, in 1919. The marriage was not meant to last, however, and the couple divorced in August 1921. Less than a year later, Vesta remarried, this time to twenty-one-year-old Dover auto dealer Harry A. Snyder (1901–1940), and the couple lived in a house on the corner of Crater Avenue and East Fourth Street in Dover, Ohio.

The New Philadelphia newspaper reported on Thursday, April 17, 1924, that on the previous evening, Harry Snyder, after returning from work, went into the kitchen to greet Vesta, who was cooking dinner at the time. Harry then went to the living room to sit and read the newspaper as Vesta finished dinner. Harry had just sat down when he heard two shots ring out from the kitchen and ran into the room to find Vesta lying on the floor. Harry ran to a neighbor's house and asked that a doctor be called at once.

Vesta was carried to the bedroom by Harry and the neighbor to await the doctor, during which time it was reported that she claimed that she wished to die. The newspaper reported that Vesta had pulled the trigger of a .38-caliber revolver three times, though only two bullets fired. One entered her hand, and the second pierced her body. Harry Snyder reported that Vesta had been depressed all day and must have gotten the gun out of a trunk in the Snyder home. Vesta was sent to Union Hospital, where she underwent surgery and, within a few days, recovered from her wounds.

Imagine the surprise of the local community when, less than a month later, the local newspaper reported a different version of events. Vesta, having recovered from her gunshot wounds, filed a report claiming that it was Harry Snyder who pulled the trigger that night. She stated that he was regularly intoxicated, jealous and violent and that he shot her after questioning her about whether she had been with another man. Vesta stated that she claimed suicide at first because she thought she was going to die and did not want to implicate her husband. An investigation was conducted, but no charges were filed against either party and the couple soon divorced.

Harry Snyder remarried, but once again his marriage ended in divorce and allegations of drunkenness and violence. Harry was eventually killed in a drunken fight in a Dover alley in May 1940. Vesta Leggett remarried in 1925; moved to Buffalo, New York; and was still married when she died in New Philadelphia, Ohio, while visiting her sister for the 1947 Christmas holiday. Vesta Leggett died on Christmas Eve 1947 and was buried in East Avenue Cemetery in New Philadelphia. Only Vesta and Harry knew for sure what happened in their kitchen the night of April 16, 1924.

1925

TRAGEDY IN NEWCOMERSTOWN: THE KILLING OF KATHRYN REED

A Pennsylvania widow started a new life in Tuscarawas County with a man she met through a matrimonial periodical. That new life was cut short on a cold December night in Newcomerstown, Ohio.

The town of Wernersville is located west of the city of Reading in Berks County, Pennsylvania, along the old Lebanon Valley Railroad. John F. Reed (1846–1922), a butcher, lived there with his wife, Mary (1855–1921), and their large family of nine children. Their children included four sons and four daughters, and one of those daughters was named Kathryn L. Reed (1887–1925). Kathryn attended school in her youth and helped keep the books for her father's butchering business.

The Lebanon Valley Railroad connected the cities of Reading and Harrisburg, Pennsylvania, and at some point, Kathryn met successful Dauphin County jeweler and watchmaker Joseph Eby (1872–1912). The two married in the fall of 1909, and Kathryn moved to Elizabethville, Pennsylvania, in Dauphin County, where Joseph operated a jewelry store and photography studio. Kathryn kept Joseph's books, as she had done for her father's butchering business. Joseph had been in ill health his entire life and, in November 1912, died from Bright's disease. Kathryn was a widow after only three years of marriage.

Meanwhile, Harvey Haver (1884–1972) and his brothers grew up working on their father Isaac Haver's (1848–1925) farm southeast of Newcomerstown, Ohio. After finishing school, Harvey pursued the painting trade while also working on the railroad. During the long days on the railroad, Harvey and his coworkers would often scan through matrimony catalogues, periodicals containing personal ads of men and women seeking spouses. It was through one of these publications that Harvey began corresponding with Kathryn Reed, now Kathryn Eby.

Kathryn and Harvey agreed to meet in Pittsburgh, and it was there that some believe the couple were married in late 1920. However, there is a marriage record in the Tuscarawas County records that indicate that they were married in April 1921. Regardless, Kathryn left Pennsylvania and moved in with her new husband in Newcomerstown, Ohio. The couple eventually purchased a home on East Canal Street in Newcomerstown and entertained Harvey's large circle of friends and Kathryn's visiting sisters often.

Notwithstanding newspaper articles noting these seemingly pleasant domestic gatherings, all was not perfect in the Haver home. Kathryn suffered from what doctors diagnosed as a heart condition, for which they prescribed the stimulant strychnine. Perhaps Kathryn, educated and used to the life of an established jeweler's wife, had a difficult time transitioning to being the wife of a simple mailman, house painter and wall paperer. Despite their disagreements, Kathryn nursed both of Harvey's parents in the last years of their lives. Regardless, the couple's frequent arguments were often the subject of gossip in the small town.

There is only one version, Harvey Haver's, of what happened the night of December 1, 1925. According to Harvey's later testimony, he arrived home from work and found Kathryn upstairs in her bed, having taken a large number of her prescribed strychnine pills. After allegedly bringing her some food, which she refused, Harvey headed downstairs to read the newspaper. Kathryn, according to Harvey, under the influence of her medication, came downstairs yelling and assaulted him as he sat in the chair. The argument ended with Kathryn dead on the living room floor.

Over a month passed between Kathryn's death and Harvey Haver placing an announcement in the local newspaper declaring that his wife was a "nagger," burned his clothing and treated him poorly. He alleged she had taken some of his money and ran off the night of November 30, 1925. Harvey claimed to not know where his wife had gone. The brief article also stated that Harvey was seeking a divorce from the wife he knew had died on his living room floor on the evening of December 1, 1925.

In the weeks before Kathryn's death, her husband, Harvey Haver, had been under investigation by the postal service for opening other people's mail. Allegedly, he was opening letters mailed to Kathryn from her sisters in Pennsylvania, among others. Apparently, Harvey had become smitten with one of Kathryn's sisters and even kissed her in the presence of Kathryn during the latter's visit to the Haver home. It was during his interrogation by authorities in that matter that Harvey told his versions of Kathryn's death.

Harvey's first version was that he had found Kathryn hanging in the basement from a chain, having died by suicide. The next version was that she had fallen down the steps and then assaulted him after taking too many of her strychnine pills. The only consistent part of Harvey's story was that, after Kathryn died, he wrapped her body with wire, put her in the trunk of his car, drove her body to his late father's farm outside Newcomerstown, threw Kathryn's body in a disused well and then attempted to convince everyone that she had run away.

Choked His Wife

—Photo by International

HARVEY HAVER,

Of New Cornerstown Village, Ohio, who broke down and confessed to Prosecuting Attorney Patrick that he had strangled his wife, and then had hidden her body in an abandoned well behind their house. Haver said she had refused to get his supper one night and that in anger he had choked her to death.

Image of killer Harvey Haver, 1926, that appeared in *The Washington Times* (Washington, D.C.), February 3, 1926. *Library of Congress.*

The authorities found Kathryn's body in the Haver well, just as Harvey relayed, and her body was sent to the coroner so that an autopsy could be performed. The autopsy's findings told a different story from what Harvey Haver had professed. There was no indication that she had hanged herself; her body showed evidence of being struck with a blunt object like a fireplace poker before her death, and there was some evidence that Harvey may have tried to burn Kathryn's body before deciding instead to put her in the well. Harvey was subsequently charged with first-degree murder by a Tuscarawas County grand jury in March 1926.

During Harvey's trial, his defense team, the local firm of Bowers & Bowers, mounted a defense that confirmed and stressed Kathryn's existing medical condition and questioned the findings of the county coroner's autopsy. It did not help the prosecution that their three separate indictments all gave differing accounts of Kathryn's murder. The four-day trial was a spectacle that attracted large crowds both inside, and outside, the courthouse. When the trial ended, Harvey Haver was convicted of manslaughter and sentenced to fifteen to twenty years in the Ohio State Penitentiary.

Kathryn Reed Haver's body was returned to her hometown of Wernersville, Pennsylvania, in Berks County, where she was buried next to her first husband, Joseph Eby. Harvey Haver spent the next fifteen years in prison before his parole in September 1941. He remarried and lived the rest of his life in Newcomerstown and Coshocton, Ohio, and when he died in 1972, no reference to his killing of Kathryn Reed Haver was mentioned.

1927
THE WELLER FARMHOUSE RAID AND A MAN OF MANY NAMES

Prior to the era of computers, fingerprint analysis and modern communication, it was often difficult to track and confirm the identities of criminals if they chose to use aliases. The story of bootlegger and illegal distiller Frank Dello (1900–?), alias Mike Brady, alias John F. Brady, alias John Robinson, is yet another example. Depending on the newspaper, the twenty-seven-year-old was from either Dover, Akron, Zanesville, Canton, Mt. Vernon or Cleveland, and no reference was made to his ethnicity. The newspaper articles also indicated that he was married, but to whom and when is difficult to determine.

During the late afternoon of Saturday, April 30, 1927, Sheriff Abe Laird (1883–1946) and his deputies, acting on tips from locals about a possible illegal still, raided an abandoned farmhouse on the Weller property off Schilling Hill Road in Dover Township. The raid completely surprised the one person manning the distillery so much that he was not even able to reach for his .45-caliber pistol sitting beside him. That man told the deputies that his name was Mike Brady, and it was under that name that he was arrested and charged with possessing liquor and implements for the manufacture of intoxicants.

According to the newspaper account, immediately after the raid, the illegal still on the Weller property was the largest that had ever been recorded in Tuscarawas County. The still was alleged to be able to produce 100 gallons of finished product every day, and in addition to the still itself, law enforcement also confiscated 120 barrels of mash, 6,500 pounds of sugar, 50 gallons of finished product and 50 empty 5-gallon containers. No sooner was Dello arrested and charged than he was released on a $2,500 bond posted by "Dover foreigners" Joseph Yarnelli and Michael Paoletti. Neither Yarnelli or Paoletti appear in records for Dover in the years before or after the event. Where the money came to bail Dello out or pay his attorneys is unclear.

While Brady's attorneys spent the next few months filing various petitions to have the case dismissed on technicalities, their client went back to work. In early August 1927, authorities in Zanesville, Ohio, arrested Dello, this time using the name Frank Dello, "alias Mike Brady," for transporting and possessing intoxicating liquor. Dello had stashed nineteen five-gallon cans of his finished product in an automobile hidden in a barn in rural Wayne Township, Muskingum County, Ohio. Dello—called the "king of the bootleggers" by the local paper—was placed in the Muskingum County Jail for failure to pay the $1,500 in fines.

His Tuscarawas County attorneys' efforts to get his case dismissed proved unsuccessful, and in early November 1927, he was transferred from the Muskingum County Jail back to the Tuscarawas County Jail to await his upcoming trial. Once back in Tuscarawas County, he was once again placed on a $2,500 bond, this time provided by the married daughter of Dover restaurateur and saloon keeper Nick Nigro. Fearing now that a jury trial might result in a long prison sentence, Dello decided to instead plead guilty to a charge of manufacturing a distilled liquor. He, still being tried as Mike Brady, was sentenced to one year in the Ohio State Penitentiary and charged a $500 fine.

The name Frank Dello does not appear in census records in the three decades after the 1927 case in Tuscarawas County—or Ohio, for that matter. The name Mike Brady does appear, however, in a few local newspaper accounts in the few years immediately following and as a head of household in the 1930 census for Dover, Ohio. Was this the same Mike Brady? The search is complicated by the fact that there was a well-known professional golfer of the time also named Mike Brady, and his name appeared in newspapers all across the country. While I do have documentation on the Brady family that appeared in Dover in the 1930 census, it is likely that you, the reader, may know more about the fate of Frank Dello, alias Mike Brady, than the historic records will ever tell us.

1930
THE DENNISON "EARLESS" MURDER

When a mutilated and unidentified murder victim turned up on a residential Dennison, Ohio street in late September 1930, authorities quickly arrested an Italian immigrant who lived nearby. The story, however, did not end with the arrest of their prime suspect—nor did the killing.

Acquaintances, Ashtabula residents and fellow Italian immigrants Joseph (alias John) Rossi (1897–1932), John (alias Tony) Scondi (1886–1954) and a "friend" ran into one another on a Steubenville street in September 1930. John mentioned to the other two that he was on his way to visit his sister Marie and her husband, Frank Marafiote (1891–1908), in Dennison. Scondi and the friend decided to come along, and the three men drank three pints of whiskey before they boarded a train for Dennison. Upon their arrival in Dennison, the trio walked a short distance to the Marafiote home on the 600 block of Grant Street.

The trio ate some sandwiches and drank beer with the Marafiotes, and at one point, Scondi went to the basement kitchen, ostensibly to wash his face. Scondi and the "friend" wanted to go to a nearby "house of ill repute," but Rossi declined and sat on the Marafiote front porch while he waited for the pair to return. Half an hour later, Scondi returned without the friend, who he said had run off somewhere. The two cleaned up and, as it was late, asked Frank Marafiote to drive them in his 1925 Model T coupe to Youngstown, where they arrived around seven thirty the next morning. The three men said their goodbyes, and Marafiote returned to Dennison.

As Frank Marafiote drove home to Dennison, George Cleary (1891–1958) was walking to work when he saw a body lying in a ditch along North Ninth

Street in Dennison just a block or so from the Marafiote home. Authorities soon arrived and determined that the unidentified body had been badly beaten with a heavy pipe and stabbed repeatedly all over; even more shockingly, the victim's ears had been cut off. One of the appendages lay on the ground next to the body along with the pipe and knife used in the killing. The investigation then began into who the dead man was and how he came to be lying, dead and earless, on a quiet Dennison street.

Robbery was quickly ruled out, as the victim's money and other valuables were untouched by his murderer. A note was found in his pocket with the name "Anthony Carbone" written on it, as well as an illegible address. The immediate theory of the victim's cause of death presented by authorities was that he was a "gangster" who had likely been "taken for a ride." The victim's identity remained unknown during the preliminary investigation, and the county coroner's death certificate merely listed the victim as an "unidentified Italian" of "about 40" years old.

The local authorities searched the area and homes in and around where the dead man's body was found, and among the locations searched was Frank Marafiote's nearby home and automobile. Located in Marafiote's basement kitchen were pipe sections that matched the type found next to the victim's body, and when authorities searched the car, they found one of the

Early twentieth-century postcard view of Dennison, Ohio. *Tuscarawas County Historical Society.*

victim's ears wrapped in a piece of newspaper and hidden behind the dash. Frank Marafiote was immediately arrested and taken to the Dennison city building for interrogation.

Under interrogation, Marafiote told of the night of the murder; the visit by his brother-in-law Joseph Rossi, John Scondi and the "friend"; and his returning the men to Youngstown without their friend. Marie Marafiote, Joseph Rossi's sister, corroborated her husband's story. The authorities were skeptical of the Marafiotes' version of events and planned to charge Frank with the murder of the unknown man. It was not until they looked into the backgrounds of Joseph Rossi and John Scondi that the case took a different turn.

Marafiote was born in Careri, Italy, and immigrated to the United States, via New York, in February 1913 aboard the SS *Mendoza*. He lived in East Youngstown (modern Campbell, Ohio) when he registered for the draft during World War I and then made his way to Steubenville, Ohio, by 1920, where he worked in a mill. It was likely there that he met Marie Rose Rossi (1900–?), sister of Joseph Rossi, before finding work in Tuscarawas County by 1923. That year, he married Marie Rose in New Philadelphia and worked as a clay miner in the twin cities of Uhrichsville and Dennison.

During their interrogation by the authorities, Frank and Marie Rose both essentially told the same story. Marie Rose's brother Joseph Rossi arrived at their home late at night with two other men, one being John (alias Tony) Scondi and the other the one they simply referred to as a "friend." They stated that the two men had left Joseph Rossi behind at the house and that only Scondi returned. Rossi, Scondi and Marafiote then took the Marafiote car and drove around looking for the friend before Marafiote drove the two men to Youngstown—a round-trip drive that took all night.

Frank could not, or would not, answer for how the victim's ear ended up in his car or how one of the pipes from his basement was allegedly used to bash in the victim's skull. However, now that authorities had the names of the two other men, their investigation expanded beyond just Frank Marafiote. After reaching out to law enforcement in Ashtabula, Youngstown and Steubenville, authorities quickly turned their attention away from Frank Marafiote as the murderer and toward Rossi and Scondi.

Joseph Rossi was a veteran of the Italian army who immigrated to the United States aboard the SS *Dante Alighieri* in February 1921 and made his way first to Steubenville, Ohio, and then to Dennison. There Rossi was involved, though not implicated in, the murder of his father-in-law in a Fifth Street home in 1924. Afterward, Rossi moved to Ashtabula, where he opened a poolroom and, in 1929, shot a sixteen-year-old he claimed attempted to break into the business. Most damning, though, was the fact that one of the aliases used by Rossi was Anthony (Tony) Carbone, the same name written on the slip of paper found in the murder victim's pocket.

Meanwhile, law enforcement was unable to locate John Scondi (1886–1954), who had gone into hiding after learning of Marafiote's earlier arrest. John Scondi, alias Tony Scondi, alias Tony Phillafroni, emigrated from Italy in 1912 and worked mostly on railroads in Pennsylvania and Ohio. At the time of the murder, he lived in Ashtabula, where he was under indictment for the fatal stabbing of a Finnish immigrant there. In the days immediately before the killing in Dennison, he was hiding in Steubenville, Ohio. Without Scondi, authorities determined to move forward with an indictment against Joseph Rossi alone.

Joseph Rossi was charged with first-degree murder, and his trial, where the prosecution presented twenty-four witnesses, began in mid-November 1930. Rossi's account of the night of the killing mirrored that told by the Marafiotes, with the exceptions that there was some disagreement about how long and where the three men later looked for the dead "friend." Marafiote had stated that Rossi carried a section of pipe with him. Rossi and Marafiote's testimony both, however, implicated John Scondi to a degree, as they asserted they knew nothing of what happened to their friend after he left the Marafiote home with Scondi. Scondi was still in hiding by the

Dennison Railyard, Dennison, Ohio, circa the early twentieth century. *Tuscarawas County Historical Society*.

time the trial concluded. After only ninety-eight minutes of deliberation, the twelve-man jury returned a verdict of not guilty on the afternoon of November 21, 1930.

After his acquittal on first-degree murder in relation to the killing of an unidentified man on a Dennison street, Joseph Rossi returned to his family and life in Ashtabula. Frank Marafiote, the original suspect in the murder, also returned to his life in Dennison. John Scondi remained in hiding, with rumors that he might be in New Jersey, Michigan or New York. Meanwhile, the murdered man was buried in an unmarked grave in an Uhrichsville cemetery, where he would not rest for very long.

In March 1931, an Italian consular agent in Weirton, West Virginia, received communication from a woman in Altoona, Pennsylvania, stating that she had not heard from her cousin in months. One of the items found on the murdered man was a numbered employee disc for the Weirton Steel Company; authorities now realized the tag matched the missing person. The body was exhumed in early April 1931 so that the cousin could possibly make an identification, and she confirmed that the man was indeed her missing cousin, Angelo Rendino (1887–1930).

Angelo Rendino was born in Foggia, Italy, in 1887 and immigrated to the United States in 1909. Once in America, he made his way west to West Virginia as a railroad laborer by 1910. Eventually, Rendino ended up in Youngstown, Ohio, and worked in steel mills there while boarding in the home of another Italian immigrant family. It was in Youngstown in July 1929 that Rendino shot and killed nineteen-year-old Samuel Armeni (1910–1929) in a duel over some slight. Rendino was indicted for murder, but he was acquitted and afterward moved to Weirton, West Virginia. When Rendino received his dagger tattoo, and whether it was a sign of any Black Hand association, is unknown.

Only a couple of weeks after the discovery of the identity of the Dennison murder victim, the Grant Street home of Frank Marafiote and his family suspiciously caught on fire and burned to the ground. The fire was investigated as arson because the authorities believed that perhaps it had been done as a warning to Marafiote now that the victim's name was known. Nothing came of the arson investigation, and no one was ever arrested in connection with the fire. Meanwhile, authorities continued to seek information on the elusive John Scondi—though he would make a dramatic appearance a year later.

John Scondi returned to Ashtabula, though exactly when is unclear, and was living in the Carso Avenue home of Lucy Catrena in early 1932. Joseph Rossi paid Scondi a visit at home on the evening of March 20, 1932, though why he went is unknown and was never ascertained. At the house, John Scondi pulled out a .38-caliber revolver and shot Joseph Rossi six times in the head and chest, killing him. Scondi turned himself in and, when questioned, stated that he had killed Rossi over a grudge—that grudge being that Rossi had implicated Scondi in the 1930 murder of Angelo Rendino in Dennison.

John Scondi was convicted of the murder of Joseph Rossi but spent less than ten years at the Ohio Penitentiary and died in 1954. Frank Marafiote relocated his family from Dennison to Weirton, West Virginia, and then eventually to Youngstown, Ohio, where he died in 1980. Why Angelo Rendino was murdered so brutally in Dennison, Ohio, in 1930 was never determined. Was it revenge for his killing of Samuel Armeni in 1929? Was it somehow related to Black Hand activity? We will likely never know the truth.

1931

JENNIE PINGLE AND THE NOTORIOUS BOWMAN BROTHERS

During the first couple of years of the 1930s, a gang led by two brothers robbed banks, grocery stores and gas stations all across southeastern Ohio, West Virginia and northern Kentucky. One of the gang's hideouts was located in the home of the estranged wife of a poolroom manager in the railroad town of Dennison, Ohio.

Greek immigrant John P. Pingle (1895–1979) arrived in the United States in 1913 and made his way west to Dennison by the early 1920s. Once there, he worked odd jobs for a few years before meeting a girl from Harrison County named Jennie C. Wright (1905–1989). The two were married in March 1925, and by 1930, they were living in a flat above a poolroom managed by John in the 300 block of Center Street. Around the same time, two brothers, Neal Bowman (1906–1934) and Howard Bowman (1910–1964), were being paroled for burglaries they committed in 1928 and 1929.

Neal and Howard wasted no time reconstituting their gang of accomplices and continuing their life of crime after their release from incarceration in 1930. They started by burglarizing homes in Harrison County and West Virginia and were suspects in a murder as well. The gang was eager, however, to branch off into higher-stakes robberies of banks and grocery stores. Meanwhile, the Pingle marriage had deteriorated, and John and Jennie were living separately by the time she and a friend met Neal and Howard Bowman's gang, now including West Virginian Lyle Cornell (1908–1975), when they passed through Dennison in early

1931. The gang holed-up at Jennie's home and, while there, planned and committed burglaries and robberies throughout the region.

Neal and Howard Bowman, along with Lyle Cornell, drove a stolen yellow Chevrolet roadster to the Indian Village Savings & Loan in Gnadenhutten, Ohio, on the afternoon of April 3, 1931. Once there, they entered the bank and, displaying three firearms to the bank president, told the manager, "We're not fooling!" After gathering up all the loose cash, they marched the staff and patrons outside, made them line up facing the wall and then hopped in their car and drove off, heading south. They had nabbed nearly $2,000 in the robbery, the equivalent of almost $40,000 today.

According to the authorities, Jennie Pingle and her friend had parked a Chrysler sedan, stolen earlier from Dennison's City Auto Company, along a rural road. The Bowman gang ditched the roadster and escaped south in the stolen Chrysler, minus Jennie and her friend. In the ensuing days, while law enforcement pursued them, they robbed more banks, grocery stores and gas stations. They even shot up the town of Georgetown, Ohio, after a robbery there, fatally wounding a bystander and adding murder to the long list of charges they would face.

Law enforcement eventually caught up to the Bowman gang as they attempted to cross the Ohio River into Kentucky. Their monthslong crime spree came to an end when the men admitted to several of the bank robberies, including the April Gnadenhutten robbery. In their confessions, the men exonerated Jennie Pingle and her friend. Despite that, Jennie and her friend left Ohio, and John Pingle filed for divorce from Jennie in November 1933, citing "gross neglect."

The Bowman brothers were found guilty and sentenced to life in prison while Lyle Cornell received a shorter sentence. The Bowmans were not out of the news yet though. Two years later, Neal Bowman convinced prison doctors he was insane and was transferred to the State Hospital for the Criminally Insane in Lima, Ohio. Around Christmas 1933, Neal Bowman escaped from the hospital, and another manhunt for him took place as he robbed his way from Ohio to Kentucky. Bowman was eventually captured in Kentucky, where he was charged with the murder of one of his accomplices.

John Pingle remarried after his divorce from Jennie and lived for many years in Uhrichsville, Ohio, where he is buried. Jennie eventually moved to Missouri, where she remarried; she died in 1989 in Nebraska. Lyle Cornwell served his sentence at the Ohio State Penitentiary, was paroled, married and lived the rest of his life in Cincinnati. Howard Bowman served a life sentence at the Ohio State Penitentiary, plotted a failed sensational prison break in 1934, died in 1964 and is buried in Columbus. Neal Bowman was put to death by the State of Kentucky for the murder of one of his accomplices in January 1936.

1931

THE MURDERS OF RUSSELL AND BLANCH SCHEIDEGER

Russell and Blanch Scheideger were walking home from the movies with their twelve-year-old son and fourteen-year-old daughter in Dennison on a cloudy Wednesday evening in November 1931. Their daughter was walking with a group of friends a good distance behind the Scheideger family when a car pulled up next to her parents and brother as they walked east on Center Street. What happened next, and in the ensuing hours, made it into newspapers all across the country.

Russell Scheideger (1895–1931) was the son of Swiss immigrant and coal miner Thomas Scheideger (1849–1911) and Ohio-born Rebecca Sprague (1850–1914). Russell grew up in the town of Mineral City, Ohio, where he lived with his parents and several siblings before moving to Dennison after 1910. There he met Blanch Copeland (1895–1931), the only child of a railroad carpenter named Thomas Copeland (1873–1933) and his wife, Lavina VanKirk (1872–aft. 1933). Russell worked as a railroad conductor, and he and Blanch married in West Virginia in November 1915.

Russell and Blanch started raising their family in a rented home on McCrea Avenue before they eventually moved into a larger home on Taylor Avenue. Russell's job as a railroad conductor, working mostly with freight, brought him in contact with people who worked in many areas of the railroad's operation. Many of the single men who worked for the railroad often boarded in the homes of other local railroaders. One such man was a fellow freight conductor of the same age as Russell named

Center Street, Dennison, Ohio, looking west, circa the 1940s. *Tuscarawas County Historical Society.*

Thomas Wheeler. Thomas had boarded in other homes in the past before being offered a room in the Scheidegers' Taylor Avenue home.

Wheeler (1895–1931) was the son of Ohio-born Isaac Wheeler (1866–aft. 1910) and German immigrant Josephine Timoiski (1868–aft. 1910). He grew up on the family's Carroll County farm with his nine siblings. He was living in Dennison and working as a brakeman for the railroad when he was drafted in the summer of 1918. He served in Europe with two U.S. Army transportation units before he returned home in the summer of 1919. After his return to Dennison, he was hired as a railroad freight conductor. It is very possible that Thomas and the Scheidegers were well acquainted before he moved into their home.

It is not clear how long Thomas Wheeler roomed with the Scheidegers before he became infatuated with Blanch Scheideger. Wheeler made frequent advances toward Blanch, some even witnessed by the Scheideger children, and Russell eventually forced Wheeler to move out of the home. Wheeler moved only two doors down the street into the home of a sister of his, but his interest in Blanch remained. Threats were allegedly made against Russell, Blanch and Blanch's brother, who also lived in the Scheideger home.

The night of November 18, 1931, Thomas Wheeler stalked the Scheideger family as they attended a movie in downtown Dennison. When the movie ended and the family began to walk home down Center Street past the railroad yard, Wheeler pulled up behind them and fired a single shotgun blast into Blanch's back, killing her instantly. Russell turned and, as he moved toward the car, was shot through the heart with a revolver Wheeler held in his other hand. The Scheidegers' son barely missed being killed himself. Wheeler drove off and, about two hours later, was found dead in his car from a self-inflicted shotgun wound.

Though there was no evidence that Blanch Scheideger and Thomas Wheeler had an affair, the newspapers depicted the tragic story as a "love triangle." Even the coroner's notes on the death certificates of Russell and Blanch referred to their deaths being attributed to "shot while walking the street over a love affair." The only fact known for sure about the death of the Scheidegers was that two children were now orphans.

1934
THE TORCH MURDER

Tuscarawas County was not immune when it came to the rise of organized crime before, during and after the era of Prohibition in the 1920s. The local newspapers carried stories of extortion, bootlegging, murder and more. During the winter of 1934, Tuscarawas County witnessed a brutal gangland killing in a style reminiscent of the worst New York, Detroit or Chicago style.

James Brick (1899–1946) and his cousin Donna Walter (1911–2003) were taking a drive on the evening of Thursday, January 11, 1934. As they drove north along Dover–Mineral Springs Road (modern Route 800) around 9:00 p.m., they were forced to slow down as they passed by two cars. One car was parked on the shoulder on their right, and the other car was parked on the shoulder on the left facing back into Dover. James noticed that a short, heavyset man was standing along the side of the car on the right-hand shoulder. Thinking nothing of it, the two continued on their way.

Fifteen minutes later, Clarence Hammell (1912–1977) and his girlfriend, having spent the evening in Dover, were returning to their homes in Mineral Springs. About four miles into their drive, they saw a 1930–32 Dodge coupe partially off the righthand shoulder, angled back toward Dover, its rear wheels in the dirt. A medium-sized man was standing next to the seemingly disabled car, and directly across the road was another car, a Chevrolet coupe. Clarence slowed down and asked the man if he needed any assistance. The man glared at Clarence and, in an accent that gave the impression he was foreign, told him to "mind your own business." Clarence, a bit startled by the response, drove on and never looked back.

Another Mineral Springs resident, Pearl Bozman (1898–?), was headed north on the same road several minutes after Clarence Hammell's run-in with the unpleasant man on the side of the road. Ahead he saw a bright light and, as he got closer, realized that a car on the right-hand side of the road was completely in flames. The car was burning within a half mile of the popular roadside resort known as the U-Auto Park. He sped on to Mineral City, where he asked Frank Riggle (1883–1996), who owned a garage in town, to call the highway patrol and report the burning wreck.

The flames that engulfed the car had more or less subsided by the time that highway patrol officers arrived on the scene. One of those officers, State Highway Patrolman Earnest P. Webb (1906–1981), examined the smoldering wreck. While he could smell that the car had been doused in gasoline or oil, the passenger compartment of the coupe was empty. Moving to the back of the vehicle, Officer Webb and others worked to pry open the rumble seat. Finally, the lid opened, and an almost completely burned body tumbled to the ground in front of the men, reeking of gasoline.

Tuscarawas County Sheriff Abe Laird (1883–1946) arrived on the scene shortly afterward, and he, along with the highway patrol and Dover police, began to investigate the area immediately around the car. It appeared that the perpetrators were trying to push the car back into the woods when it became stuck in the mud. Spots of blood were noticed on the pavement around the vehicle, leading to speculation that the victim may have been lured to the location and subsequently murdered there. As witness reports came in, law enforcement began to suspect that this murder was connected to some form of organized crime activity.

While the body had been burned so badly that at first glance it appeared to be nothing but a torso, some of the victim's belongings were discovered in the mud around the vehicle. Among them were some keys, a belt buckle with the letter J on it and a single-bladed pocketknife. One of the keys, perhaps providing a clue, had the name of a Cleveland key making shop on it. This information led local law enforcement to believe they could identify the victim, and officers from Cleveland arrived the next day to investigate and confirm.

A few days earlier, a lifelong criminal associated with organized crime racketeering in Cleveland had been reported missing by his family. His abandoned car had been found under the Harvard-Dennison Bridge in Cleveland at the beginning of January. His name was Frank T. Joiner

(1885–1934), and he had been in trouble with the law his entire life, including burglary, attempting to break his children out of reform school, abandonment and, lately, racketeering. Joiner had run Cleveland's notorious Harvard Club, and he was the only eyewitness to the gangland murders of Joe Porrello and Salvator "Sam" Tilocco at the Venetian Restaurant on July 5, 1930.

As the investigation continued, law enforcement were also able to determine that the torched coupe had, at one point, been owned by murdered Cleveland criminal and bootlegger Joseph Orsino (1898–1933). Orsino was murdered in March 1933 by two men who, as he exited a Cleveland store, opened fire on him at point-blank range with shotguns. The clues, evidence and witness reports all leaned to the burned body being the missing Frank Joiner, but the victim's true name was not learned until late the next day.

Newspapers across the state of Ohio had already run the story naming Frank T. Joiner as the likely victim of the "torch murder" when a woman in Canton became concerned about her own husband. She had not seen her husband since the day before, the day of the murder and torching, and had begun to reach out to her husband's friends and associates inquiring about his whereabouts. Her effort ended abruptly when the police arrived at her home on a tip that her husband was the owner of the burned-out vehicle found in Dover.

Carmela Gioffre's (1887–?) husband, Joseph Gioffre (1888–1934), had dropped her and her daughter Candida (1913–?) off at downtown Canton's shopping district the afternoon before at around two o'clock. The two planned to shop and take in a movie at the Valentine Theater while her husband worked. Joseph had not returned home that night, but that was not unusual for him given the nature of his work and did not immediately worry Carmela. Meanwhile, the investigators working to identify the nearly cremated remains found in the torched Dodge coupe in Dover had managed to trace the ownership history of the car. This led them to Carmela's doorstep the following afternoon of January 12, 1934.

After being contacted by police in Canton, Carmela and her daughter were brought to New Philadelphia to try to identify the objects that had been found at the crime scene. Carmela identified the belt buckle as being that of her husband, and later that day, Sheriff Laird confirmed that the keys found were to the locks on Carmela and Joseph's home at 1011 Fifteenth Street Northwest in Canton. Now that the authorities had a positive identification on the torch murder victim, they set out to discover who he was and why someone would want him dead.

Artist's rendering based on a period newspaper image of victim Joseph Gioffree, 2024. *Courtesy of Luc Poirier.*

Joseph Gioffre, sometimes recorded as Joffre, was born in Italy under the name Giuseppe Gioffre. Little is known of his early years in Italy except that he was born on May 4, 1888, the son of Dominic and Maria Gioffre, and married Carmela in Italy around 1910. The couple had a daughter, Candida, in 1913, around the time Joseph immigrated alone to the United States. Like many immigrants before him, Joseph planned to earn enough money to bring his family at a later date. It was how Joseph earned his money that ultimately led to his murder, and subsequent burning, on a road outside Dover in 1934.

Joseph traveled to Detroit, Michigan, after his arrival in the United States, settled in a predominately Italian neighborhood and found work in the auto industry. It was here that he began to be associated with Italian organized crime, often referred to in the papers of the day as Camorra or the "Black Hand." Joseph succeeded in bringing his family from Italy in 1924, and they settled in a small house at 15750 Linwood Street in Detroit. The tentacles of Detroit's organized crime operation began to spread out into the cities of northern Ohio, and Joseph soon followed, moving his family to Mansfield, Cleveland and, finally, Canton.

Everywhere Joseph Gioffre lived, his connections with organized crime activities and personalities were documented by arrests and investigations. Extortion, bootlegging, murder and violence against businesses that refused to cooperate were his calling cards. His closest associates were known members of organized crime throughout northern Ohio, though the police were not able to obtain convictions for any of the crimes for which they were accused. Canton police had even raided Gioffre's home, searching for evidence in an extortion investigation, but turned up nothing. The police believed that, at the time of his death, Joseph Gioffre was the head of Canton's organized crime operations.

The day of his murder, after dropping off his wife and daughter, Gioffre visited a "bootlegging place" in Canton in the company of fellow Canton resident Louis Marino. Marino, in July 1933, had been the victim of an attempted murder in his back garden. Though he survived, he refused to identify his attacker and no one was ever charged. Gioffre received a telephone call around 4:30 p.m., and he and Marino left the "bootlegging place" shortly after. They drove to the home of another associate, Peter Poro, and arrived at his home on Cherry Avenue in Canton around 5:00 p.m.

Joseph Gioffre, after he and Marino arrived at Poro's home, made a phone call to an unknown associate. According to Poro, the conversation was conducted entirely in Italian, though Poro was unable (or unwilling) to state what the conversation was about. Numerous neighbors of Poro then witnessed Joseph Gioffre leaving the home and driving away in the Dodge coupe around 5:30 p.m. Neither Peter Poro nor Louis Marino were able (or willing) to say where Gioffre was headed or with whom he had spoken to on the phone. It was the last time Joseph Gioffre was seen alive.

According to the pathologist who performed the autopsy on Gioffre, Joseph was killed by a blow to the head that fractured his skull. The pathologist believed, because of the condition of Gioffre's heart, that he had been killed shortly before being mutilated, stuffed into the back of the coupe and set afire. Blood spatter found alongside the road near the coupe supported the idea that Gioffre had been murdered near the car. The murder likely had occurred only minutes before witness James Brick first saw the two cars at 9:00 p.m. The pathologist reported Joseph Gioffre's manner of death as "evidently a gangster murder."

No one was ever brought to justice for the murder of Joseph Gioffre a few miles outside of Dover, Ohio, on the night of January 11, 1934. Authorities chalked up the murder to a disagreement among organized crime parties over some aspect of their illicit activities. All indications are that, after the death of her husband, Carmela returned to Italy with her daughter. Tuscarawas County was not immune to the dangers of organized crime. The Black Hand had been around the county for decades before Gioffre's killing, but the brutal and dramatic death of Joseph Gioffre in 1934 was unique in the county's criminal history.

1934
A DUCK'S DEATH AND A BRUTAL MURDER IN MINERAL CITY

Ralph Bowman (1900–1971) and Edward Rudolph (1900–1934), born in Mineral City, Ohio, in 1900, grew up as friends in the tight-knit community shaped by the coal and clay industries. Despite their shared background, their lives took a dark turn, culminating in a fatal altercation in 1934 over a duck, forever changing their destinies.

When the two registered for the World War I draft in 1918, Ralph was working for the B&O Railroad while Edward worked for the Huff Run Coal Company. During the ensuing fifteen years, both men worked in the clay and coal industries that were commonplace in Mineral City.

The work was hard, and the two young men were known to indulge in drinking heavily, an activity that brought them frequently into conflict with law enforcement. Ralph Bowman was often arrested for public intoxication, disorderly conduct and the occasional assault and battery. In addition to being drunk and disorderly, Edward was arrested and charged in 1926 with contributing to the delinquency of two minor girls who he arranged to "work" in Canton. A few years later, he was also involved in a drunken altercation with another man that led to Edward being stabbed. Needless to say, Ralph and Edward were not model citizens.

Two years after Edward pleaded guilty to the delinquency charges, he married, in March 1928, Viola Daily (1910–1933). The couple had already had a child in 1927, so it would seem the marriage was one of convenience or obligation. Regardless, the couple were separated by the time the 1930 census was taken, with Viola living with her family and Edward living with

View of Mineral City, Ohio, circa the early twentieth century. *Tuscarawas County Historical Society.*

his. Edward then married again, this time to divorcée and mother of three Edna Martin (1894–?) in West Virginia in November 1931. Ralph Bowman, on the other hand, had yet to marry and was living with his family in Mineral City when the 1930 census was taken.

By the fall of 1934, Edward and Ralph had become neighbors in Mineral City and by all accounts socialized and drank together regularly. Edward lived in his home with his wife and three stepchildren while Ralph lived in the house next door. Like many people in rural early twentieth-century Ohio, both households supplemented their purchased food with their own gardens, chickens and ducks. No one could have suspected that something as simple as a drunken argument over a random duck would dramatically end Edward and Ralph's friendship.

Ralph and Edward were drinking heavily on the evening of September 12, 1934, when the discussion led to Ralph's anger over Edward's ducks getting into his garden and eating his vegetables. Ralph angrily picked up one of Edward's ducks and, with a pocketknife, killed the bird in front of Edward. Furious, Edward struck Ralph in the face, knocking him to the ground. Ralph got up, still holding his knife, and slashed Edward across the throat, severing his jugular vein. Edward bled to death in the yard, and Ralph was arrested and charged with first-degree murder.

Ralph Bowman went on trial in November 1934, and after fifty minutes of deliberation, a jury of four women and eight men found him guilty of first-degree murder but recommended life in prison instead of the death penalty. Bowman spent the next twenty-nine years at the Ohio State Penitentiary before being paroled in 1963. Once released, Bowman returned to Tuscarawas County and was frequently arrested for drunkenness and disorderly conduct. Ralph Bowman was found lying in the street in front of his Tuscarawas Avenue home, dead, in October 1971. One man's life ended, and another was ruined, because of a drunken argument over a wayward duck. Both Edward Rudolph and Ralph Bowman are buried in the Mineral City Cemetery.

1936

AN AFFAIR IN BEARTOWN: THE KILLING OF FRANK MEYERS

The Charnock family lived on both sides of the Ohio River, sometimes in Ohio and sometimes in West Virginia, during the latter half of the nineteenth century. Myrle Charnock (1894–1981), born during a time when the family lived on the West Virginia side, was the daughter of William (1839–1922) and Mary (1851–1921) Charnock. The Charnock family were living on a Green Township, Harrison County, Ohio farm near Hopedale by the time they were recorded in the 1910 United States Census.

Meanwhile, Howard K. Duvall (1895–1941) was living with his family in Washington Township, Carroll County, Ohio. Howard was one of nine children (five sons and four daughters) of farmer William (1875–1941) and his wife, Amy Duvall (1866–1962). Howard was working as a miner when he met Myrle Charnock from neighboring Harrison County, and the couple married in December 1915. Two years later, they lived in Flushing, Ohio, in Belmont County, where Howard worked as a coal miner for the North Belmont Coal Company.

The Duvall family included three sons by the time they settled in the neighborhood of Beartown, just north of Dover, in the 1930s. Howard Duvall moved on from mining and was now in the trucking and junk business, as well as taking on odd jobs here and there. The family even took in boarders now and again for some additional income. Howard Duvall had become a widely known junk dealer throughout Tuscarawas County by the time his marriage took a turn for the worse.

Recently, a Millersburg man had purchased a strip coal mine outside of Strasburg, Ohio, and hired a man from Killbuck, Holmes County, to oversee

Killer Howard K. Duvall, early 1930s. *Courtesy of Randall Duvall.*

it for him; that man was named Frank (sometimes Frantz) Meyers (1880–1936). Somchow the married Meyers met Myrle Duvall, and they struck up a romance that caused the Duvalls to live separately by the fall of 1936. Howard Duvall rented a room in Dennison while Myrle lived in the family home with the sons in Beartown. Howard and Myrle, in competing petitions, both asked for a divorce by the beginning of December 1936.

On the night of Tuesday, December 29, 1936, Howard Duvall, accompanied by a friend, drove to the Duvall residence in Beartown. When he entered the home, he found Myrle and Frank Meyers on the sofa in the living room. Depending on the witness statement, Howard either already had a stick in his hand or picked up a log from the fireplace. He then struck Frank Meyers in the head repeatedly with it. Frank fled outside with Howard following, continuing to rain blows on his head. Frank collapsed into the mud in front of the house, badly injured. Howard and his friend fled the scene before Frank was eventually taken to Union Hospital.

Frank Meyers died two days later on December 31, 1936. Howard hid out for several days, leading to a manhunt, before turning himself in on January 4, 1937. Initially charged and indicted for first-degree murder, the question of whether Howard had entered the Duvall home already armed or had armed himself with a fireplace log after entering became a vital point of contention. One indicated premeditation while the other did not. Eventually, believing they could not prove premeditation, county prosecutors convinced Howard Duvall to plead guilty to manslaughter. Howard Duvall served two years before being paroled in 1939 and died from a brain tumor two years later in 1941. Myrle Duvall eventually remarried, lived in Strasburg and died in 1981.

1936
UNRAVELING THE MURDER OF WILLIAM MOORE

During the Great Migration, a period of American history when millions of Black southerners moved to find work in the industrialized cities of the North, many found themselves in the town of Newcomerstown, Ohio. This is the heartbreaking story of one of those men.

According to U.S. Census records between 1920 and 1940, the Black population in and around Newcomerstown hovered around two hundred men, women and children. Many of those families lived in rented homes on what was then called Clow Avenue (now called Martin Luther King Drive) in Newcomerstown. Where Clow Avenue joined with State Street to the north there was a club room for Black residents, while on the southern end of the street there were churches that catered to the Black community.

Many of these Black residents had come from southern states and were now working at the James B. Clow and Sons Radiator and Water Pipe Foundry. One of these men was a man named Jack Russell (1890–1956), who had migrated with his family from Alabama to Newcomerstown around 1927. Jack rented a home on Clow Avenue, and he frequently hosted his neighbors and friends there. One of those friends was a Kentucky-born man, William Moore (1880–1936), who worked for the Works Progress Administration (WPA).

One night in late January 1933, Russell and Moore attended a party with some other neighbors. Following the gathering, a disagreement between two of the men led to a fight that ended in the death of one. The killer then disposed of the dead man's body in the Tuscarawas River to try to hide his crime. Russell, his wife, Moore and the killer were all arrested, but following a confession from the killer, the others were released. This case influenced law enforcement's thinking when Moore himself was killed three years later.

While many of the Black residents of Newcomerstown lived with their families on Clow Avenue, many of their neighbors one street over to the east on South College Street were the families of White workers of the Clow Foundry. This physical closeness, along with the fact that men from both streets worked together at the foundry, led to many interactions outside of the foundry itself. While newspapers from this period are quiet regarding outward hostility toward Black Newcomerstown residents, not all of those interactions were positive.

William Moore attended a gathering of neighbors at Jack Russell's home on Clow Avenue on the evening of March 31, 1936. The party included Moore, Moore's friend Warner Seymour (1875–1941), Willie "Blue" Owens (1913–?), Albert Ridley (1911–1967), Jack Russell and Jack's daughter. Jack's wife, Elizabeth Russell (1906–1935), died a year earlier from tuberculosis. William Moore had some drinks but stayed at the gathering for only about an hour, leaving at around 10:30 p.m. in what the other attendees stated was an intoxicated state.

William Moore never returned to his boardinghouse or to work. A search and investigation were begun to discover what had happened to him. Law enforcement received some tips about a vehicle being driven down to the

Main Street, Newcomerstown, Ohio, 1907. *Tuscarawas County Historical Society.*

Tuscarawas River that night, and indeed some tracks were found. They searched the river and its banks, including dragging the river near the location of the automobile tracks. It was nearly a month later that William Moore's body was discovered lying on the banks of the Tuscarawas River two miles west of Newcomerstown. Initially, his death seemed like it was an accident, but after an autopsy revealed blunt force trauma to the head and chest, a murder investigation was begun. All eyes turned to the men at the March 31 gathering on Clow Avenue.

One January evening in 1933, three years before William Moore's killing, some men on Clow Avenue got together for a gathering at the home of Tennessee native Lester Seay (1898–1970). The party included William Moore, Jack Russell and his wife and father and son Sam (1889–1933) and Albert Ridley. Seay and the elder Ridley got into an argument that turned physical, and Seay struck Ridley in the head with a doorknob. According to Seay, Ridley then started stumbling toward the direction of the Tuscarawas River. Ridley's body was found there, dead, the next morning.

Moore, the Russells and other witnesses told the story during an inquest held by the county coroner in the days after the body was found. Seay, later that year, was indicted by a grand jury for manslaughter for Ridley's death. He went to trial in June 1933 and was found guilty and sentenced to one to twenty years in the Ohio State Penitentiary. Seay was granted parole two years later and returned to Tennessee. This crime, so similar in outward appearance to William Moore's 1936 death, led local authorities to believe it had once again been a disagreement between Black residents of Clow Avenue and nothing more.

Needless to say, when Moore's body was found along the Tuscarawas River in a similar condition, and under similar circumstances, as Sam Ridley's, the authorities turned all their attention to the men at Jack Russell's party. At this point, the investigation was being handled primarily by Newcomerstown law enforcement at the direction of the town's mayor, Charles B. Mugford (1884–1939). Tuscarawas County officials, including Sheriff Abe Laird (1883–1946), were kept at an arm's length during the initial investigation.

One of the challenges during the investigation was determining the motive for killing William Moore. By all accounts, all of the men attending Jack Russell's gathering on the evening of March 30, 1936, were friends. Yes, the men had been drinking, but they all reported that the party was a pleasant one. Moore lived a simple life alone in a rented house with very little needs other than food and drink. When his body was found, the money from his recent pay was still in his pockets. Regardless, the investigators took Willie Owens and Albert Ridley into custody, and later another man named Jasper McCall (1908–1973) was also held. All of the men were held without charge.

Sheriff Abe Laird, who at the time was running for the Ohio State Senate, was not content to allow Newcomerstown officials to investigate the case on their own. Laird and his deputies began their own investigation in May 1936 and interviewed many of Moore's neighbors and friends in the neighborhood south of the James Clow factory. Laird, not willing to assume that Moore had been killed by one of the other partygoers at Jack Russell's home, interviewed White residents of the neighborhood as well. Within a month of beginning his investigation, Laired had cracked the case.

Sheriff Laird brought one of Moore's Newcomerstown neighbors who lived on South College Street, Richard Carpenter (1878–1950), to New Philadelphia for questioning in early June 1936. During that questioning, Carpenter confessed to killing Moore and implicated two other men: Moore's friend Warner Seymour and Carpenter's friend Albert V. "Red" Baker (1883–1974). It was now up to Laird to determine what happened the night of March 30, 1936, that led to Moore's death.

After Sheriff Abe Laird took Richard Carpenter, Albert V. "Red" Baker and Warner Seymour into custody, the men told their version of the events of March 30, 1936, that led to the killing of William Moore and the subsequent dumpling of his body on the banks of the Tuscarawas River. It was a story that shocked the small community south of the James B. Clow and Sons Radiator and Water Pipe Foundry in Newcomerstown, Ohio.

Richard Carpenter's wife, Clara Mae (1892–1962), was pregnant at the time of Moore's death, and according to the three men, an intoxicated William Moore left Jack Russell's party and made his way to the residence of Richard Carpenter to see the mother of his coming child. William Moore was the actual father of Clara Mae's child, not Richard Carpenter. Warner Seymour, knowing this, followed William in an attempt to stop him. Whether Richard knew the situation before William arrived at his home is unclear, but a heated argument ensued between Moore, Carpenter and Baker.

When Moore and Seymour arrived at the Carpenter residence, Richard and Albert Baker were waiting for them. It is possible that it was during this confrontation that Richard Carpenter became aware that William Moore was actually the father of the child his wife was carrying. Richard had armed himself with a stick or board and Albert was holding a large rock. A scuffle between the men took place, during which William Moore was struck across the head and chest by Carpenter and Baker. One blow to the chest, directly over Moore's heart, killed him.

At first, the men placed Moore's body in a coal shed for over a week before deciding to dump it in the Tuscarawas River. All three men were charged with murder and pleaded not guilty, and the case was sent to a Tuscarawas County grand jury in late June 1936. After testimony, including that of Clara Mae Carpenter, all three men were released without charge. The jury determined that the murder of William Moore had been justified given the situation. A later grand jury would try to indict Albert Baker separately for the murder, but that also failed. The killers of William Moore went free.

Richard and Clara Mae Carpenter divorced a year later and moved away from Tuscarawas County, but the family stayed together. Richard died in February 1950, and Clara Mae Carpenter is recorded in his obituary and census records as his widow. The child of Clara Mae and William Moore, raised by Richard and Clara Carpenter, died in a car accident in 1973. She was a mother of three children at the time. Albert Baker lived in Tuscarawas County for the rest of his life and died in Uhrichsville, Ohio, in 1974. Warner Seymour moved to Stark County, Ohio, shortly after his acquittal, where he died in 1941.

William Moore, like many Black southerners, followed the Great Migration north to Ohio in search of work and a better life. He found work and friends in a tight-knit community in Newcomerstown, Ohio. His killing, and the subsequent acquittals of his killers, shined light on a culture that viewed some acts as being even worse than murder. Whether the child of William Moore and Clara Mae Carpenter was ever told the truth of her parentage, or if it was obvious to others, is impossible to know.

1945
FORGOTTEN IN A DITCH: THE HERGOVICH MYSTERY

Tuscarawas County farmer Charles Montan (1888–1976) was on his way to a nearby farm sale on the afternoon of March 12, 1945, when he decided to walk along a railroad right-of-way located between Kaserman's Lane and the Brown Coal Company's Red Onion Coal Mine in Beaverdam Valley. As he walked along, he noticed a form lying in a nearby ditch. It was a man's body, partially clothed and obviously deceased. As soon as he could, Montan notified the county sheriff's office, and Sheriff John McIntosh (1901–1948) and his men soon arrived at the scene.

When the sheriff arrived, he took a closer look at the individual and noted that he was clothed only in long underwear, a striped shirt and socks. No other clothing was noted immediately around the body. The body was in a crouched-like position with its arms crossed over the lower part of the chest. There was a combination of animal predation on the body as well as significant decomposition despite the fact that the area had been mostly covered with snow since mid-December. The body was then taken to be examined by Tuscarawas County Coroner Dr. D.M. Ceramella (1909–1999).

Dr. Ceramella determined that he did not have the facilities and expertise to positively identify the body, so he sent the body to be examined at the Cuyahoga County Morgue by their coroner, Dr. Samuel R. Gerber (1896–1987). Dr. Gerber was able to suggest a cause of death—drowning—and lift fingerprints off the badly decomposed body. Those fingerprints matched those of a man who had applied to work at a munitions plant in Ravenna during World War II. The man's name was Mike Hergovich (1885–1945). Authorities now had a name to add to their investigation.

Mike Hergovich was born in the Croatian portion of Austria-Hungary in November 1885 and immigrated to the United States in 1906. He at first settled in western Pennsylvania before relocating to Milwaukee, Wisconsin, possibly with a younger brother, for a short period around the time of World War I. Hergovich moved to northeastern Ohio before 1920 and started working for the Universal Sewer Pipe Company, sometimes in Portage County and other times in Tuscarawas County. He never married and was a fireman at the company's Goshen plant at the time of his death.

Mike Hergovich was last seen in the company of a couple that he had occasionally boarded with, Alvin Murphy (1905–1965) and his wife, Mary, at the home of Fred Seibert (1908–1948), where they played cards with another man, Jack Newton (1902–1948), on the evening of January 13, 1945. Mrs. Murphy stated that she last saw Hergovich the next morning when he left with Seibert and Newton. Despite Dr. Gerber's determination that Hergovich drowned, Prosecuting Attorney Arthur B. Cunningham (1905–1973) remained convinced that he had suffered foul play.

Lie detector tests were administered to six unnamed suspects—but likely including the above—by Cleveland police detective David Cowles (1897–1988). The results absolved all six of his death and disappearance. Mike Hergovich was buried in the East Avenue Cemetery in New Philadelphia, Ohio. Three years later, one of those men, Fred Seibert, died by suicide and another, Jack Newton, died in a mining accident. That same year, Sheriff McIntosh died in an automobile accident. What really happened to Mike Hergovich remains a mystery to this day.

1947
THE COMPLICATED DEATH OF LILLIE GROVES KAMBAN

The death of Lillie Groves Kamban, mother of eight, in June 1947 was a headline in the local newspaper, and the story of how and why Lillie died was fodder for the papers for the next several days.

The Groves family can trace their Ohio roots to the arrival of William Groves and his two brothers to Belmont County in 1800. One of the brothers had a son named William Groves (1805–aft. 1880), born in 1805 in Belmont County. William married a young woman born in Virginia named Nancy Watson (1802–1870) in 1826 in Belmont County, and the couple had at least three children before they moved to Adams Township, Coshocton County, by 1850. One of those children was a son named Joseph Groves (1832–1873), who married Mary E. Albert (1841–bef. 1888) in November 1859 in Coshocton County, Ohio.

Joseph and Mary resided in Adams Township, Coshocton County, and there raised their own family of at least four children, two daughters and two sons. One of their sons was named Albert Groves (1868–1950); he had made his way into Tuscarawas County by the time he married Salenah Wilson (1868–1952) in August 1888. The couple settled down in Oxford Township in Tuscarawas County, just outside the town of Newcomerstown. There they raised three children, including a daughter named Lillie Groves (1906–1947).

Marko Kamban (1895–1981) was born in Montenegro, the son of Suto Kamban and his wife, Maria Lubarda. After Marko turned seventeen, he immigrated to the United States along with three other men, two of whom also carried the last name of Kamban. When Marko arrived in the United States in April 1912, he claimed to be twenty-one years old on the passenger list. Shortly afterward, he made his way to Belmont County, Ohio; changed his name to Martin; and found work in the numerous mines in the region. He settled in Cambridge, Guernsey County, by 1918 and there married fellow immigrant Julia Serota (1903–?). The couple had three children before divorcing around 1926.

Meanwhile, Lillie Groves had started working as a house cleaner, and somehow that work brought her to Cambridge in the late 1920s, where she met Martin Kamban. The couple married in Guernsey County, Ohio, in May 1929 and lived in Guernsey County and Noble County until eventually moving to Tuscarawas County by 1945. During the years 1930 to 1940, Martin and Lillie's family grew with the arrival of eight children, and occasionally, children from Martin's previous marriage also lived with the family.

It was after the family moved to Tuscarawas County that Lillie, and perhaps Martin as well, met another local man named John Meek (1912–1991). Meek was the unmarried son of a Perry Township, Tuscarawas County farmer who passed away suddenly in 1918 from appendicitis. After his father's death, John and his two siblings lived with their mother, who tried to continue to work the family farm near the crossroads of Peoli in Tuscarawas County. The family eventually moved to Newcomerstown, where one of her sons worked for the railroad while John worked in the neighborhood as a farm laborer.

Victim Lillie Groves Kamban and an unnamed child, circa 1930. *Courtesy of Andrew Kamban.*

It became apparent that all was not well in the Kamban family when, in early April 1945, Martin sued for divorce from Lillie. The newspaper report of the suit stated that Martin charged Lillie with infidelity and alleged that she neglected the family's eight children. Martin went even further by naming the man he alleged with whom Lillie had been having her affair. According to Martin, that man was John Meek. While the couple reconciled, Lillie's relationship, whatever it was, with John Meek ended with her death on the road in front of her farmhouse two years later.

No one can be certain why Lillie Groves Kamban was standing in the road in front of her home in Peoli at 10:10 p.m. on June 5, 1947. At that moment, she was struck by a car driven by family acquaintance John Meek before being hit a second time by a vehicle that was driving behind Meek's. After seeing that Meek did not stop, the second driver followed Meek, stopped him and forced him to return to the scene. Authorities were then called, but by the time they arrived, Lillie was already dead.

The investigation into Lillie's death began immediately, and Meek was taken to nearby Newcomerstown for questioning. Meanwhile, Lillie was turned over to the Tuscarawas County coroner. The coroner determined that Lillie's skull had been fractured by a blow to the head from being struck by the vehicle driven by John Meek. During the initial investigation, it was determined that Meek and Lillie knew each other, so the coroner, at the time of his review of Lillie's injuries, could not determine if her death was accidental or intentional.

While it was clear that Meek's car fatally struck Lillie, something Meek later admitted to, just why Lillie was in the road at ten o'clock at night was still in question. Prosecutors investigating Lillie's death interviewed "persons involved in the case" while the sheriff's office visited Peoli and questioned residents and the Kambans' neighbors. One must assume that one of those interviewed was Lillie's husband, Martin Kamban. The only version of events that could not be told to investigators, tragically, was Lillie's.

During interviews conducted by authorities with thirty-five-year-old John Meek, it became clear to them that perhaps John was not entirely competent. John had worked as a farm laborer in the local community, had never married and still resided with his parents at the time of Lillian's death. It was further learned that John was sixteen years old when he was in the sixth grade in Gnadenhutten, indicating that perhaps he was a slower learner than most children his own age. All of these things, and perhaps more, led to the court deciding to have a competency hearing prior to pressing any charges against Meek.

One thing that obviously must have come up in the investigation was Martin Kamban's April 1945 divorce filing in which he claimed that Meek and Lillie were having an affair. This assumption, and whatever else the authorities learned from the investigation, led to their conclusion. They determined that Lillie and Meek's affair had continued into 1947; that she was in the road that night to warn Meek not to visit her, as she had guests; and that Meek had not seen her in the road before striking her. Ultimately, they determined that Lillie's death was an accident.

The case concluded when John Meek pleaded guilty in late June 1947 to the crime of leaving the scene of an accident and was sentenced to six months in the Columbus workhouse. Meek died in Newcomerstown, Ohio, in October 1991, having never married. Martin Kamban eventually remarried in 1960 and died in Dennison, Ohio, in May 1981. Lillie Groves Kamban was forty years old at the time of her death on the road in front of her home in Peoli, just down the road from where she now lies buried.

1948

A LIFE NEVER LIVED: THE KILLING OF LUCILLE LYNCH BAKER

Lucille was fourteen when she arrived in Dover, Ohio, from Tennessee to stay with her uncle's family. She was seventeen when she married, eighteen when she became a mother and nineteen when she died. This is, without a doubt, one of the hardest stories to tell. Hardest because Lucille seems to have been forgotten and hardest because living family members and associates of the people involved may be hearing this story—or at least this version—for the first time.

Lucille "Roxie" Lynch (1928–1948) was the daughter of Curtis Lynch (1909–1986) and Marie York (1911–?), both of Waynesboro, Tennessee. The marriage did not last long, and the couple divorced shortly after Lucille's birth in 1928. Marie and Lucille went to live at Marie's parents' home, where she was recorded as living in the 1930 census. One year later, Marie married Work Projects Administration (WPA) worker Barney C. Skelton (1892–1974), and by 1940, the couple had moved into a home near her parents, where they had three children, all daughters.

Lucille was around fourteen years old when she moved from Waynesboro, Tennessee, to live with her uncle's family in Dover, Ohio. What precipitated Lucille's move to Ohio in 1942 is unknown. Lucille's uncle Thomas York (1900–1971) worked at the Reeve's Manufacturing Company and raised his large family just west of Dover off the Dover-Sugarcreek Road. One of the Yorks' nearby neighbors was the family of mechanic Walter Baker (1894–1986) and his wife, Pearl (1906–1967). One of their sons was named Roy Harold Baker (1926–2017).

Artist's rendering based on a period newspaper image of murderer Roy Baker, 2024. *Courtesy of Luc Poirier.*

There's little about Roy's childhood in the historical record, but sometime in the 1930s, he and his older brother went to live with their paternal grandfather on Union Avenue in New Philadelphia, Ohio. The older brother was already working as a laborer in 1940 at the age of seventeen, and two years later Roy dropped out of school to go to work as well. He was working at the Marsh Wall Products Company in Dover when he registered for the draft in 1944 and was drafted two months later.

After completing basic training, Roy was assigned to a machine gun squad in the Forty-Second Infantry Division. He arrived in the European theater just in time to take part in the Allies' defense of the Ardennes Forest, the "Battle of Bulge" as it came to be known. Roy's position was overrun, and he was taken prisoner by the advancing Germans. Roy spent the next six months as a prisoner of war, digging ditches for his captors and losing forty-five pounds in the process. He was liberated in early June 1945.

Roy returned to Dover after his discharge from the army and found work at the Reeves Steel and Manufacturing Company. He also worked part time for a local boxing promoter and sporting goods store owner named Paul Cash (1912–1983). It is possible that Roy met Lucille while she was working as a waitress at the Wayt Restaurant on West Third Street in Dover. The twenty-year-old Baker asked seventeen-year-old Lucille to marry him, requiring her to petition the court to allow her marriage as a minor.

Roy and Lucille were married on February 9, 1946, and the couple moved into a home on Race Street in Dover. Nine months later, the couple welcomed their first child, a son. Roy continued working at the Reeves plant, often working the overnight shift, while also assisting Paul Cash with arranging local boxing matches and occasionally working at the sporting goods store on the corner of Factory and West Third Streets that Cash operated with his partner. There was no indication at that time that Lucille would be dead from foul play only a year and a half later.

The source material for what Roy H. Baker and Paul Cash initially claimed to have occurred in the Baker home the night of April 6, 1948, comes from the publicly reported testimony and statements by Baker, his employer and friend Paul Cash and their attorneys. A later grand jury also heard testimony from the men, but what was said in court at that time is unavailable.

According to Roy, around 10:00 p.m., tension flared between Lucille and him in the front room of their Dover home. The argument allegedly revolved around Lucille's refusal to engage in intimate relations, escalating into a physical altercation. Roy, in a fit of anger, said that he struck Lucille, causing her to fall to the floor. The commotion didn't go unnoticed, as concerned neighbors reported hearing screams emanating from the Baker residence at the time. Roy claimed that he then helped Lucille up after the altercation and mentioned that she appeared dizzy. Roy noted that Lucille was wearing a blue housedress during this disturbing incident. Shortly after the altercation, at around 10:30 p.m., Roy said that he kissed Lucille and their eighteen-month-old son goodbye and left for his night shift at Reeves Manufacturing, leaving the aftermath of the quarrel behind.

Paul Cash claimed that, at around midnight, he called the Baker residence trying to reach Roy. Cash stated that when Lucille answered the phone, she was seemingly hysterical and informed him that she had fallen down the stairs trying to rush to pick up the phone. Concerned, Paul hurried to the house and once there found Lucille conscious but quickly slipping into unconsciousness. Now, rather than the blue housedress, Cash stated that she was wearing pajama bottoms, a sweater and ankle socks.

Paul contacted Reeves Manufacturing around 12:25 a.m. to let Roy Baker know about Lucille's fall and her condition. Roy was immediately driven home by a coworker and discovered Lucille lying unconscious on the daybed in the front room. Roy and Paul then summoned a doctor to assess Lucille's condition. The doctor determined that she needed to be taken to the hospital, and at 1:35 a.m. she was admitted to Union Hospital in Dover.

It was quickly determined that Lucille was comatose from her head injuries, and tragically, Lucille never regained consciousness. She succumbed to her injuries at 11:30 a.m. on April 9, 1948, just days after the violent altercation and the alleged fall down the stairs. The cause of death was attributed to a subdural hemorrhage and head injury, and the county coroner ordered an autopsy performed. The results of that autopsy called into question Roy Baker and Paul Cash's version of events.

Within a few days of the autopsy being performed, Roy and Paul's story started to look less and less likely. The coroner determined that Lucille's injuries were inconsistent with a fall down the stairs and believed, rather, that foul play was involved. The autopsy also determined that at the time of Lucille's death, she was six weeks pregnant. Shortly after, Paul Cash was charged with first-degree murder, and Roy Baker was held in custody as a material witness. Questions still remained, though, and things would quickly change.

The local Tuscarawas County newspapers at the time of Lucille's death reported that Paul Cash was a well-known boxing promoter, the American Athletic Union Commissioner for Tuscarawas and Coshocton Counties and a partner in a sporting goods store at the corner of West Third and Factory Streets in Dover. Little else about his past was reported by the newspapers at the time, but that past was what made him a prime suspect in Lucille's death.

Paul Cash was born in Follansbee, West Virginia, just south of Steubenville, Ohio, in 1912, the son of a steel mill worker. Paul was very athletic and found himself on numerous sports teams for the steel mills where he worked in his youth. He was amateur boxing by the time he was seventeen years old in the Steubenville area and elsewhere. Cash eventually decided to become a boxing promoter instead and demonstrated his showmanship when he sold tickets to his public wedding to a local girl in the fall of 1933. Not surprisingly, the marriage did not last long.

The next time that Paul Cash saw his name in the local newspaper, it was August 1935. Paul, his father and a brother took part in the beating and eventual death of another player at one of the Wheeling Steel League's softball games. Paul's father threatened to beat another person with a bat when another player, a Black man named Lawrence Jones (1897–1935), interceded (Lawrence Jones was the father of the well-known Steubenville football player Calvin Jack Jones). The Cash sons then set upon Jones with their fists and bats; others joined in before eventually chasing Jones off a nearby ridge. Jones fell down the hill and broke his back and would die just a few days later. Paul Cash was given a seventy-five-dollar fine and a suspended sentence.

Shortly after this incident, Paul moved from Steubenville to Buffalo, New York, and found work there while continuing to promote boxers and becoming the director of the Strip Mill Athletic Club. While in New York, Cash also remarried, marrying Dorothy Timoshuk (1921–2010) around 1939. Two years later, Cash was in the news again, this time after several complaints about him being a "peeping Tom." Cash pleaded guilty and was sentenced to six months in the Erie County Penitentiary and fined fifty dollars. Shortly after his release from prison in New York, Cash moved his family to Tuscarawas County.

Paul Cash, his wife, Dorothy, and their two sons arrived in Tuscarawas County in the early 1940s. Paul quickly became involved in local athletics, partnered with a local billiard hall operator and also began managing up-and-coming local boxers like Wally Unsold (1923–2003). Not long after he arrived, Paul was already in trouble with the law when he and his partner, not surprisingly given their business, were fined for violating Dover's gambling laws. Paul Cash did not keep a low profile.

There is no way to know exactly how Paul Cash met Roy Baker, but at the time of Lucille's death, Baker was working part time for Cash while working full time with Reeves Manufacturing. Whether Baker worked at the sporting goods store or aided Cash with his various boxing promotions is unclear, though he may have been doing both. Despite Cash's violent and criminal history, he would soon find himself no longer the prime suspect in Lucille Lynch Baker's death.

When a *Columbus Evening Star* tabloid reporter wrote two stories the week of April 19, 1948—"Scan Night Love Shift" and "Triple-Deck Love Affair Turned Up by Investigators"—the public got its first glimpse into what may have really happened to Lucille Lynch Baker the night of April 6, 1948. Paul Cash was more than just Roy Baker's employer, if he ever was even that, and what happened to Lucille was far more violent than a single strike or a fall down the stairs.

The tabloid article and petitions from Paul Cash's attorneys finally managed to shake loose the unreleased autopsy report conducted by Tuscarawas County Coroner Demetrio Ceramella, MD. The autopsy report confirmed much of the tabloid's story, including the fact that Lucille had been beaten all over her body, not just her head, and that she was around six weeks pregnant at the time of her death. The tabloid also reported on another, previously unreported item: Lucille and the married Paul Cash were having an affair.

The autopsy report certainly showed that Roy Baker had been less than straightforward about his altercation, and assault, on Lucille prior to him going to work on the evening of April 6, 1948. It also called into question Paul Cash's story about calling the house to speak with Roy and that Lucille was conscious when he arrived at the house later that evening. There was also the mystery of what happened to the dress that Roy claimed Lucille was wearing before he went to work. Roy claimed his mother had taken it to clean it, but when? Between him leaving for work and Paul Cash arriving at the home at near midnight?

Paul Cash's charges were reduced to second-degree murder, and he was freed on an $8,000 bond; meanwhile, Roy Baker was feeling the heat brought on by the release of the autopsy report and the tabloid's articles. A week later, in early May 1948, Baker confessed that he knew about the affair, knew Lucille was pregnant, beat her far worse than he first admitted and that she had not fallen down the stairs. This confession contradicted all of Paul Cash's statements about the phone call and the fall down the steps, and prosecutors insisted that Cash must still face charges. If nothing else, Cash had conspired with Baker to conceal the real cause of Lucille's death.

The grand jury was reconvened and heard Roy Baker's confession, Paul Cash testified further and Tuscarawas County Coroner Ceramella presented the full results of the autopsy. What precisely was said in the testimony is unknown, grand juries being secret, but when it was finished, Roy Baker was charged with first-degree manslaughter and the indictment against Paul Cash was dismissed. A few days later, Baker pleaded guilty to the charge and waited to learn his punishment.

Roy H. Baker was sentenced on May 13, 1948, for having killed his pregnant nineteen-year-old wife and the mother of his child, Lucille Lynch Baker. Baker received a one- to twenty-year sentence in the Ohio Reformatory in Mansfield. According to Baker's attorney, Roy's reaction (beating his wife to death) was "a natural reaction of a young husband… when he learned that she was unfaithful." Baker was paroled on May 18, 1949, having served just over one year in prison. That was what passed for justice for Lucille Lynch Baker in 1949.

1954

THE MIDVALE HATCHET MURDER

Midvale, Ohio youth Delbert Sherrell's (1944–1961) grandfather sent him to check on a neighbor on Sunday, February 7, 1954. The previous night, the family had heard loud arguing coming from the neighbor's shack on Eastport Road and became concerned when they had not seen the neighbor all day Sunday. When Delbert looked into the shack, he saw a man's body lying on the floor, motionless. Concerned, Delbert's grandfather decided to call the authorities. Deputy Sheriffs Clyde Morris (1903–1977) and Don Patterson soon arrived at the scene.

The neighbor who lived in the shack was a World War I veteran named Albert "Bertie" Carpenter (1890–1966), who had been in trouble with the law before. Albert stabbed a man to death in 1927, served one year and later drew a gun on a courthouse clerk in 1950. In both cases, his actions were attributed to too much drinking rather than any propensity for violence. Regardless, the dead man lying on Albert's floor with a dozen hatchet wounds to his head was not Albert Carpenter. It was Albert's younger brother James Ralph "Miney" Carpenter (1907–1954).

Albert and James Carpenter were the sons of William Carpenter (1862–1944) and his wife, Margaret Jennie Pollack (1866–1939), originally from Kimbolton, Ohio. The family moved to Tuscarawas County before 1900, living first in Mill Township and then in Midvale. There were four sons and a daughter in the Carpenter family, and one of those sons died in 1922 from tuberculosis contracted while serving overseas during World War I. Albert was the oldest son, James the youngest.

The deputies investigating learned of the fighting that was heard the night before James's body was found and immediately began to try to locate the shack's owner, Albert Carpenter. They discovered that he had stopped by the Arnold Grill, where he called a cab to take him to New Philadelphia. The cab driver, Ray Thompson (1927–1960), stated that he had dropped Albert off near the Reeves Hotel. New Philadelphia police were notified, and they made their way to the hotel to determine if Albert was still there.

Artist's rendering based on a period newspaper image of murderer Albert Carpenter, 2024. *Courtesy of Luc Poirier.*

New Philadelphia Police Chief Emery Gintz (1889–1980) and Patrolman Harley Shaffer (1908–1954) arrived at the hotel around 10:30 a.m. on Monday, February 8, 1954, and discovered that Albert Carpenter was indeed still lodging there. They took Carpenter into custody and transported him to the county jail. Carpenter denied any knowledge of the murder of his brother and claimed that his brother "Miney" had thrown him out of the shack after they had argued. An attorney from the county prosecutor's office was called to formally interview Carpenter at the jail.

During that interview, Albert Carpenter's story changed dramatically, and he confessed to having murdered his brother. According to Albert, the two were arguing about Albert's drinking and Albert's request to borrow James's automobile. According to Albert, James knocked him down and kicked him, after which Albert noted that he said to James, "You son-of-a-bitch, I ought to kill you." Albert claimed he then picked up the hatchet and struck James "three or four times" with it. That Albert Carpenter killed his brother James was now a fact, but why Albert truly did so still remained a mystery.

The question of what caused Albert "Bertie" Carpenter to brutally murder his younger brother, cleaving his skull with several blows from a hatchet the night of Saturday, February 6, 1954, was still unanswered. Albert's assertion that they argued over his drinking and borrowing a car did not seem to warrant Albert's murderous reaction. The question needed to be answered by law enforcement and prosecutors before presenting their case to a Tuscarawas grand jury. Albert's penchant for drinking was obviously well-known, but there was apparently something else that needed to be considered as well.

When Albert was younger, he worked in the Robinson Fire Clay Products plant in Midvale. Albert suffered two traumatic injuries while working there before he was twenty-one years old. When Albert was eighteen years old, he was steam cleaning the boiler flues when a steam hose became dislodged and scalded the entire lower part of his body, burning his flesh below the ribcage and almost proving fatal. Three years later, while walking past a piece of large, belted machinery, a heavyweight belt broke and struck Albert in the head. Albert was knocked unconscious for a time by the force of the hit and suffered a large gash in his head. A doctor was called for, and ostensibly, Albert recovered from his head wound.

When World War I began, the nearly twenty-eight-year-old Albert submitted a claim to be exempt from service due to his occupational injuries. His claim was denied, and he was drafted and entered service in September 1918. Albert served stateside, first in a supply unit and later in an engineering unit, before being discharged in December 1918. It was following these two accidents and Albert's military service that Albert's name began to appear in the local newspapers for issues related to heavy drinking.

On the afternoon of Sunday, November 7, 1927, Albert got into an altercation with two other men in front of Earl Gribble's (1902–1979) poolroom in Midvale. During the fight, Albert sliced the jugular vein of a twenty-eight-year-old man named Julius Boyer (1897–1927) and nearly removed the right eye of another man named Hollie Stone (1907–1980). The altercation was allegedly over a sum of no more than five dollars. For some reason not stated in the paper, Carpenter's friends and family requested that he be given only parole for Boyer's killing. The judge at first agreed but then changed his mind after the dead man's friends and families demanded jail time for Albert. Albert served one year at the Ohio Penitentiary for manslaughter and was released in May 1928.

Albert Carpenter lived with his parents and worked odd jobs, including mining and janitorial work. It was sometime after the death of his mother in 1939 and his father in 1944 that Albert moved into the shack in Midvale. Albert's next major run-in with law enforcement occurred in the spring of 1950, when he drew a revolver on a courthouse clerk while looking for copies of his parents' estate papers. While he was taken to jail, there is no evidence that he was ever charged with a crime resulting from the incident.

After the hatchet murder of his brother James four years later, prosecutors sought second-degree murder charges, but the grand jury decided to indict him for first-degree murder. Albert's attorney, the prosecutor and the judge all seemed uncomfortable with the indictment and asked that Albert be examined by doctors at the Massillon State Hospital to determine his mental state and competency. A month later, two doctors certified that Albert was "incurably insane," and the judge ordered him to spend the rest of his life at the Massillon State Hospital. Albert Carpenter died there in April 1966 and is buried in East Avenue Cemetery in New Philadelphia with the rest of the Carpenter family.

Was it the trauma of Albert's two accidents as a young man that led to his heavy drinking? Did the blow to Albert's head contribute to his drinking and, later, mental instability and antisocial and violent behavior? These are questions we will never know the answers to.

1958

A GRISLY DISCOVERY: THE UHRICHSVILLE BONE CRATE

Two boys were spending their New Year's Day in 1958 off from school exploring behind the old Herrick house on Trenton Avenue in Uhrichsville, Ohio. Next door to the house was the Martins Ferry Glove Company's building and some other smaller buildings as well. The boys made their way into one of them, an old shed, and among the various equipment stored there they found an old crate. In the crate, wrapped in burlap, was a startling discovery: bones of all types and sizes, including what was obviously the bones of a human hand.

One of the boys grabbed a couple of the larger bones, and the two boys went home to show their parents what they had found. After showing the bones to one of the boy's fathers, Elmer Voshall (1900–1975), they were told to return the bones to where they had found them. Afraid to go back to the barn, they disposed of the bones on a nearby railroad track instead. Meanwhile, they had told another boy of their find, who then told his parents about the mysterious box of bones. That boy's father called Deputy Charles Malterer (1930–1977).

Deputy Malterer, accompanied by Uhrichsville Patrolman Frank Mathus and Deputy Sheriff Clyde V. Morris (1903–1977), visited the shed and located the crate full of human remains. They noticed two items of particular interest. First, while the box contained a number of bones, there was no skull, and second, there was also a local newspaper in the box dated 1941. The officers turned the crate over to the coroner, Phillip Doughten (1921–2019), so that he could examine the bones and decide how old they were and perhaps the sex. The officers then began their investigation.

Postcard image of Third and Main Streets, Uhrichsville, Ohio, looking west, 1907. *Tuscarawas County Historical Society.*

Their investigation took a number of directions over the next several hours, including considering that they may be the remains of a vagrant who went missing around the same time as the 1941 newspaper or whether the bones had been used in the past by a local doctor in his studies. The coroner noted that the bones still had some flesh and muscle attached and that the lack of a skull made him question whether a doctor would have used them as a study tool. Ultimately, for reasons unknown, they also discounted the newspaper as having any connection to the bones themselves.

Investigators decided to interview Jessie Herrick (1880–1958), the widowed wife of the late local newspaper editor Volney Herrick (1877–1925), about whether she had any idea how the bones ended up in a shed that had once been a part of their property. According to Mrs. Herrick, she recalled that during the lifetime of Dr. Joseph Haverfield (1852–1917), an unidentified man was struck by a train and his body was discovered a short time later. The local medical society dissected his body, and she remembered that Dr. Haverfield had buried the bones in a nearby orchard.

Phone calls to Dr. Haverfield's grandson in Florida were made by investigators to see if they could confirm Mrs. Herrick's story. The grandson told the authorities that "he vaguely" remembered a box of bones that he thought had been buried in a nearby orchard and possibly dug up later. Despite the fact that the coroner concluded that the crate contained the bones not of one person but of a man, woman and child, authorities closed the case, content that the crate found by the boys was likely Dr. Haverfield's. A question remains unanswered by the investigation to this day. Where did the bones of the woman and child come from? We will likely never know.

ABOUT THE AUTHOR

Noel B. Poirier is a historian, writer and nonprofit executive who resides in New Philadelphia, Ohio. Noel has worked in the public history field for over thirty years, leading history museums and libraries, helping tell the stories of communities across three states. He has written for numerous national and regional history publications, presented at countless libraries and museums and believes in the power of local history to connect us with the larger American experience.